LEADER GUIDE

Avery T. Willis, Jr.
Kay Moore

LIFEWAY PRESS
NASHVILLE, TENNESSEE

ISBN 0-7673-3558-9

Dewey Decimal Classification: 248:83

Subject Heading:YOUTH-RELIGIOUS LIFE//CHRISTIAN LIFE

Unless otherwise noted, Scripture quotations are from the Holy Bible,

New International Version, copyright © 1973, 1978, 1984

by International Bible Society.

Scripture quotations marked AMP are from *The Amplified Bible* © The Lockman Foundation 1954, 1958, 1987.

Used by permission.

Scripture quotations marked GNB are from the *Good News Bible,* the Bible in Today's English Version.

Copyright © American Bible Society 1976. Used by permission.

Scripture quotations marked NASB are from the NEW AMERICAN STANDARD BIBLE,

© Copyright The Lockman Foundation, 1960, 1962, 1963, 1968, 1971, 1972,

1973, 1975, 1977, 1995. Used by permission.

Printed in the United States of America

LifeWay Press

127 Ninth Avenue, North

Nashville, Tennessee 37234

CONTENTS

THE AUTHORS

AVERY T. WILLIS, JR., the author and developer of *MasterLife,* is the senior vice-president of overseas operations at the International Mission Board of the Southern Baptist Convention. The original *MasterLife: Discipleship Training for Leaders,* published in 1980, has been used by more than 250,000 people in the United States and has been translated into more than 50 different languages. Willis is also the author of *Indonesian Revival: Why Two Million Came to Christ, The Biblical Basis of Missions, MasterBuilder: Multiplying Leaders, BibleGuide to Discipleship and Doctrine,* and several books in Indonesian.

Avery served for 10 years as a pastor in Oklahoma and Texas and for 14 years as a missionary to Indonesia, during which he served for 6 years as the president of the Indonesian Baptist Theological Seminary. Before assuming his present position, he served as the director of the Adult Department of the Discipleship and Family Development Division, the Sunday School Board of the Southern Baptist Convention. He and his wife, Shirley, have five grown children. They experienced 19 straight years of having teenagers in the home and now are relating to their 10 grandchildren, three of whom are teenagers.

KAY MOORE served as the coauthor of this updated edition of *MasterLife.* She was formerly a design editor in the Adult Department of the Discipleship and Family Development Division, the Sunday School Board of the Southern Baptist Convention. A writer, editor, and conference leader, Moore has authored or coauthored numerous books on family life, relationships, and inspirational topics. She is the author of *Gathering the Missing Pieces in an Adopted Life* and is a frequent contributor to religious magazines and devotional guides. She and her husband, Louis, live in Richmond, Virginia and have a teenage daughter and a son in college.

INTRODUCTION

MasterLife is a sequential developmental, small-group discipling process to help Christian students master life by developing personal, lifelong, obedient relationships with Jesus Christ. This Leader Guide provides step-by-step guidance for facilitating group studies for *MasterLife, Student Edition,* in the *MasterLife* process. By studying this Introduction, you will learn how to disciple believers using *MasterLife*.

THE MASTERLIFE PROCESS

MasterLife was written to help youth believers make the following definition of *discipleship* a way of life:

> Christian discipleship is developing a personal, lifelong, obedient relationship with Jesus Christ in which He transforms your character into Christlikeness; changes your values into Kingdom values; and involves you in His mission in the home, the church, and the world.

Participants in *MasterLife, Student Edition* study learn how to deepen their relationships with Christ through a 14-week discipleship process that consists of the following sections:

- *MasterLife, Student Edition,* Introductory Meeting
- *MasterLife, Student Edition,* The Disciple's Cross—Weeks 1-6
- *MasterLife, Student Edition,* Growing Disciple's Workshop
- *MasterLife, Student Edition,* The Disciple's Personality—Weeks 7-12
- *MasterLife, Student Edition,* Testimony Workshop

Each section builds on the other and is a prerequisite for the one that follows. Students will benefit most and gain valuable information and experiences to be disciples of Christ if they complete all of the sections.

The student book employs an interactive learning process. Each day for five days a week, students are expected to study a segment of the material and complete related activities. Each day's work should require 20 to 30 minutes of study time.

The *MasterLife* process involves six essential elements. These elements are like the chair pictured.

1. The *daily activities* in the student book leads members into a closer walk with Christ. Doing these exercises daily is important.

2. The *weekly assignments* in "My Walk with the Master This Week" are real-life experiences that will change their lives.

3. The *leader* is a major element. Discipleship is a relationship. It is not something members do by themselves. Members need human models, instruction, and accountability to become what Christ intends for them to be. That is why Jesus commanded His disciples to make disciples (see *Matt. 28:19-20*). We all need someone who has followed Christ long enough to challenge us. To become better disciples, students need a leader to whom they can relate personally and regularly. Members will not accomplish the goals for *MasterLife* without you to teach them, model the behavior, and hold them accountable.

4. The weekly *group sessions* help students reflect on the concepts and experiences in *MasterLife* and help them apply the ideas to their lives. The group sessions allow students to experience in their inmost beings the profound changes Christ is making in their lives. Each group session also provides training for the next stage of spiritual growth.

5. *Christ* is the Discipler, and students become His disciples. As they fully depend on Him, He works through each of the previous elements and uses them to support members. If any element is omitted, the discipling process will not be effective.

6. The body of Christ—the *church*—is vital for complete discipling to take place. Students depend on Christian friends for fellowship, strength, and ministry opportunities. Without the church, youth members lack the support they need to grow in Christ.

As the leader, make sure all the elements are included. Without any one of these essential components students will not experience *MasterLife*. Although students may benefit from completing the studies on their own, they will have missed the critical element Jesus' disciples experienced: relationships with one another in Christ's presence.

STEPS FOR STARTING A *MASTERLIFE* GROUP

1. *Pray.* Seek God's direction as you determine whether He wants you to lead a *MasterLife* group. Enlist a prayer partner to pray with you. If God so leads, then proceed with the next steps.

2. *Secure approval.* If you are a layperson, consult with your pastor or an appropriate church-staff member before scheduling a *MasterLife* group in your church. Provide the pastor or staff member copies of the student book and Leader Guide. Make sure this person understands the process, course goals, content, and procedures.

3. *Select leaders and provide training.* Use "Optional Leader Training" on pages 14-17 in this Leader Guide to offer leader training in your church. Also, area *MasterLife* conferences are offered throughout the year that will renew and broaden your view of discipleship. You will be better prepared to lead in discipling believers. You will be introduced to resources designed to help believers grow in Christ. These conferences are well worth the investment of your time and energy. To learn about these training opportunities, contact the Youth Section, Discipleship and Family, MSN 152, 127 Ninth Avenue, North; Nashville, TN 37234-0152; (615-251-2855).

4. *Set a time, date, and place.* Allow the group to set the best time and place to meet. Consider one of the following options.

Option 1: Conduct group sessions in students' homes. If you move from one home to another each week, be sure that hosts do not compete to serve the best refreshments. Offer simple refreshments before or after the session. Plan a short break without extending the meeting. Begin and end each session on time.

Option 2: Schedule group meetings for the same place each week. If you meet at church, check the church schedule to make sure a distracting activity is not scheduled for a room nearby. (See "How to Lead a Small Group," p. 12.)

5. *Recruit members.* Compile a list of names of students you would like to participate. (See "How to Select Students to Disciple," p. 9.) Pray about these prospective members and begin contacting them. If you plan to recruit youth church-wide, schedule at least a four-week period to register students and promote the *MasterLife* group. Promote through announcements in church publications; on bulletin boards; and through testimonies in worship services, Bible-study classes, and youth discipleship groups. Visit each prospect personally, if possible. (See "Enlisting Disciples," p. 9.) If possible, invite prospective group members to minister and witness with you before the study begins. Make certain the group you enlist consists of no more than 10 people. There are drawbacks to larger groups:

- allowing each person to participate each week is difficult
- accountability decreases because you do not have time for all members to report to the group
- you cannot give personal time to members
- you will have more dropouts

If you have more than 10, create another *MasterLife* group or establish a waiting list for the next cycle of studies.

6. *Order materials.* Order one student book for each participant at least six weeks in advance of the starting date. *MasterLife* resources with item numbers include:
- *MasterLife, Student Edition* (ISBN 0-7673-3495-7)
- *MasterLife, Student Edition Leader Guide* (ISBN 0-7673-3558-9)

All materials listed are available from the Customer Service Center; 127 Ninth Avenue, North; Nashville, TN 37234; 1-800-458-2772.

7. *Set fees.* Members should purchase their own books unless

the church has decided to subsidize the cost. Students should pay at least part of the cost to invest in *MasterLife*. Charge an additional fee if you need to fund related costs of this study.

8. *Get started.* Read this Leader Guide, and read *MasterLife, Student Edition* before the Introductory Session.

A BIBLICAL MODEL FOR MAKING DISCIPLES

Many people think that disciples are made as they sit in a classroom or take a course. If that is your concept of making disciples, you are in for a surprise. Consider the following factors that support a biblical model of disciple making.

• *Make disciples even though your life is crowded with priorities.* Jesus made disciples in one of the busiest schedules imaginable. Often, He did not have time to eat, rest, or sleep. In a normal 24-hour day, He probably had less discretionary time than you do or than the busiest person you know does. Every day multitudes of people surrounded Jesus. He often took His disciples aside to rest, reflect, teach, and prepare, but people continually interrupted them. Most of the time Jesus was discipling on the go.

Time is the most important commodity in today's technological environment. That means we must prioritize our time. It means we will be willing to change our schedule when we realize that the Lord wants us to help a disciple. It means we must make discipling others a priority. As you begin to lead a youth *MasterLife* group, prioritize your time and be willing to change your plans when a disciple needs help.

• *Disciple making requires intentionality.* We must focus on making disciples in the fast lane. Otherwise, we lose sight of the main task Christ has given us—the Great Commission. *Matthew 28:19* literally means, "As you go, make disciples." Paul also discipled on the go (see *2 Tim. 2:2.*) He did not stop everything and make disciples. Paul made disciples as he lived his life—even in prison!

• *Disciples are not instantly made.* Regardless of new technologies and advanced teaching methods, developing disciples is much like physical development. It cannot be rushed. Discipleship takes time.

• *Use everyday situations as opportunities to make disciples.* Jesus made disciples when He was interrupted, was asked questions, was challenged by His enemies, was faced with problems, was dealing with evil spirits, and was pressed by adoring crowds. Jesus took advantage of everyday situations to disciple others.

• *Always relate disciples to the Father.* When we make disciples, we are relating God to people and people to God. At this juncture disciples are made. This means we can seize the opportunity at the crowded intersections of life and relate how God is involved. We can bring God's perspective to bear on the situation and help disciples follow God's leadership in solving problems. The greatest discipling takes place when a disciple faces a crisis. Then he or she is most teachable.

DISCIPLESHIP IS A RELATIONSHIP

Discipleship is a relationship and a process. No program or fixed structure can be designed that produces disciples.

Discipleship is not a course. Often, discipleship is defined as content. Some people think they make disciples when they teach certain material. Content is important, with the Bible as the first source of revelation. However, many people believe that if they communicate certain facts, a person is discipled. Even doctrine—a vital part of discipleship—is not sufficient. Studying every discipleship course available does not in itself make someone a disciple. Jesus said, *"The scribes and the Pharisees have seated themselves in the chair of Moses"* (Matt. 23:2, NASB). Jesus agreed that these persons were orthodox. He followed this assessment with [They] *"do not do according to their deeds: for they say things, and do not do them"* (Matt. 23:3). In the Great Commission Jesus said, *"Teaching them to obey everything I have commanded you"* (Matt. 28:20). Jesus went beyond knowing the commands to doing them. Discipleship involves practicing His commands.

In *John 17* Jesus revealed His heart in the last prayer with His disciples before He went to the cross. Jesus stressed that as the Father had related to Him, He had related to the disciples. In this relationship Jesus taught them God's Word but also urged them to obey the Word. He taught and prayed for the disciples. We disciple persons in relationships with Jesus Christ, not in a body of knowledge.

Discipleship is not a program or a method. No one way of discipling persons works with everyone. Although you can use a sequence or a process of growth that is logical or developmental, we cannot prescribe a step-by-step procedure that will be effective for everyone. So, how can we use *MasterLife, Student Edition* to disciple others? Picture *MasterLife, Student Edition,* as a tool that relates persons to Christ, who disciples them. Use it to help disciples relate to Christ in a personal way and to become obedient to Christ. *MasterLife, Student Edition,* teaches obedience in many ways, including the completion of weekly assignments. If members do not honor their covenant with the *MasterLife* group or prioritize their time to do the assignments, remind them that obedience is an attitude of the heart, not just a response to direct commands of Scripture.

Since discipleship is based on relationships, our relationship with participants is a key factor in making disciples. We need to remain flexible and to make time to develop a personal relationship with each group member. How? Take students with you as you minister or work. Be ready to disciple during ministry times, recreational outings, and family situations.

God seeks personal, obedient, and lifelong relationships. Help students focus on developing relationships with Christ that continue to grow long after the study ends.

Relate all teachings to students' relationships with Christ. For example, relate each discipline of the Disciple's Cross to a relationship with Christ. When you talk about spending time with the Master, emphasize a daily quiet time. When you talk about living in the Word, show how that allows God to communicate with us. When you talk about praying in faith, show how prayer deepens our relationships with Christ. When you talk about fellowshipping with believers, show how the body of believers helps reveal Christ and brings us into closer relationship with Christ. When you talk about witnessing to the world, emphasize that it is witnessing to Christ in your life. When you talk about ministering to others, show how ministry in Jesus' name recognizes our relationship with Him.

HOW DISCIPLING TAKES PLACE
As someone who has responded to Christ's call to discipleship, you are not only sent by Christ to reconcile persons to the Father but are also commissioned to make disciples. Look at Jesus' example to learn ways you can disciple other believers.

Jesus used spontaneous occasions to disciple persons. These persons were discipled simply because they happened to be there. But Christ also entrusted His vision to an even more select group.

To the twelve men God gave Him, Jesus spoke most openly and urgently about His mission. Jesus invested most of His time in them. The Father gave these men to Jesus with two purposes in mind: that they should be with Him and that He might send them forth (see *Mark 3:14*). He chose them according to the Father's leadership and then invested His life to train them. Not only would they carry out His mission, but they would also multiply by making other disciples.

What can we learn from Christ's method that will help us

with our discipling task? Jesus met people's needs where they were—in large groups, small groups, and as individuals. The DiscipleLife Strategy is a church growth model for youth ministry based on the pattern of discipleship established by Jesus with His disciples. The DiscipleLife Strategy will help you build an intentional ministry of discipling teenagers.

• *Crowd discipling.* Assist students in their discipleship growth simply because circumstances have brought you together. Examples of crowd settings are when all teenagers in your church plus their friends, visitors, and prospects come together. This meeting can focus on discipleship, recreation, and music; or it could be a short-term study such as a DiscipleNow experience.

• *Group discipling.* All teenagers in a church could be part of a weekly, small-group, continuing study of discipleship material or it could offer a short-term growth study.

• *Core discipling.* An intentional discipling process for the teenagers at church because of their personal commitment. *MasterLife, Student Edition,* is an example of indepth group study. Sequential discipling may occur in a group or in a one-to-one relationship. In either case, you help those you disciple reach specific goals and a specific maturity level.

• *Individual discipling.* These teenagers desire personal or one-to-one discipleship. An apprentice learns skills, behavior, knowledge, and attitudes from someone who serves as a mentor. This occurs when a person who has expertise in a certain area such as teaching, preaching, or ministry gives a student on-the-job training in that area. The person grows as a disciple and learns how to disciple.

YOUR ROLE AS A DISCIPLER
Our role in disciple making is to challenge teenagers to hear and respond to Christ's call to discipleship. When a person has responded, our role is that of mentor, helper, leader, teacher, counselor, and friend in that person's spiritual growth. Four roles indicate how we relate to those we assist in their discipleship growth.

• *Servant.* Avoid feelings of superiority or specialness. Remember that the student has responded to Christ's call. Therefore, the student is Christ's disciple, not ours. Our role as discipler is that of a servant. Remember that Christ Himself said that He had come to serve and not to be served (see *Matt. 20:28;*

Mark 10:45). Our greatest joy is to help the student be successful.

• *Spiritual parent.* We do not cause growth; God does. We do all we can to facilitate that growth. We minister to students at the point of their needs. We appeal to others to demonstrate more maturity. We encourage others to *"grow up into him, who is the Head, that is, Christ" (Eph. 4:15).*

• *Steward.* As we approach our task of making disciples, we are to be wise master builders who build on the foundation of Christ (see *1 Cor. 3:10; 4:1).* We assess where teenagers are in their spiritual development and give them the right kind of help. If they are new believers, we start them on the basics of *Survival Kit for Youth, Revised.* We lead them into the church's continuing discipleship program while we work with them personally. This type of training provides the broad base for discipleship that specialized assistance cannot. The person is guided into *MasterLife* training and later into multiplying ministries.

• *Encourager.* At every stage of development disciples need encouragement. Encouragement creates the right conditions for disciples to grow to their potential.

HOW TO SELECT STUDENTS TO DISCIPLE

Just as the Father directed Jesus to the disciples He had chosen, carefully make your selection with God's leadership. You can never be sure that you have chosen well until you see the kind of fruit a disciple produces. Here are ways God may direct you to the ones He has chosen for you to disciple.

1. *Pray.* Ask God to direct you to the disciples He has chosen for you.

2. *Evaluate them in many situations.* Note how they respond to advice or help. People reveal their character as they react to everyday as well as stressful situations. However, do not make this the determining factor. For one reason or another we probably would have eliminated all of the twelve Jesus chose.

3. *Answer these questions:*
• Does this teenager desire to know and follow God?
• Does this teenager relate well and serve others?
• Do you and this student have similar goals, values, and priorities for Christ and His kingdom?
• Is this teenager faithful in all he or she does?

• Can this teenager teach others?
• Is this teenager available for the amount of time required?

4. *Avoid making exceptions for certain teenagers just because you like them.*

ENLISTING DISCIPLES

Disciples can be enlisted in a number of ways. Here are some ways to enlist disciples.

1. *Love them.* Jesus loved His disciples so much that they gladly followed Him. Many will respond to the love you show them. Take a personal interest in them. They will be drawn to you and to Christ in you.

2. *Serve them.* Jesus served His disciples; He even washed their feet. Do not demand that others serve you. Servants attract disciples who serve others.

3. *Spend time with them.* Love often is spelled T-I-M-E. When you genuinely love teenagers, spending time with them is a priority.

4. *Have something in your life that they need.* Students want to become disciples when they see qualities in the discipler that they want but do not have. What kind of life attracts disciples?
• A life totally committed to Christ
• Someone who "has it all together"—a whole, well-adjusted person with strength of character
• Persons who stand for something and who live what they profess
• A person who has an effective ministry and who can show others how to have the same
• A person who has something in common with the disciple
• Someone who has a good home life
• Persons who integrate their spiritual and secular lives

5. *Lead them to Christ.* This is the most natural way to begin a discipling relationship. Continue to disciple the teenager until traits of a multiplying disciple develop.

6. *Recruit them to a vision rather than to a program or an organization.* The Master and His vision need to motivate disciples. The *MasterLife* process is a means to an end—a vehicle that takes a disciple from one point to another. Share the vision God has given you for your part in His divine plan. Give others opportunities to share your vision as you serve together.

7. *Personally enlist them.* Tell what God has done in your life through *MasterLife*. Draw the Disciple's Cross to explain how God has helped you as a disciple. Explain the requirements of being in a *MasterLife* group. Be frank about the type of commitment required. Refrain from asking for an immediate answer. Ask them to pray about it and receive direction from God. Ask them to contact you when they have decided. If they have not contacted you in a week or two, contact them.

DEVELOPING COMMITMENT IN DISCIPLES

Common questions surface about participation in *MasterLife*. How do you get students to be committed to Christ and to develop as disciples? How do you develop a commitment that motivates them to continue a personal, lifelong, obedient relationship with Christ? Our goal is to make disciples who will continue to apply the principles and live the Christlike lifestyle long after they complete course requirements. Here are ways to help disciples be committed.

1. *Involve disciples in what you are doing.* Let disciples see how you respond in your own lifelong, obedient relationship with Christ. If Christ has first place in your life, how does that commitment express itself in the way you serve on church committees, visit sick or homebound persons, lead your Bible-study class or discipleship group, visit prospects, or participate in your church's prayer ministry? Do you treat others differently and speak to them differently because you are Christ's disciple? Do you stick to your commitment even when other events demand your time? Ideally, disciples will see a commitment to Christ that is not dislodged by other priorities.

2. *Get involved in what teenagers are doing.* Showing an interest in others communicates a servant heart.
   • Meet them on their turf, as Jesus did when He visited in Peter's home when his mother-in-law was ill (see *Mark 1:29-31*). Doing this demonstrates your commitment. It shows that you care enough about them to enter their worlds and involve yourself in their day-to-day struggles.
   • Meet them at their work, recreational activities, school (if possible), as Jesus did when He visited Peter at his fishing trade (see *Luke 5:1-11*). Not only does this enable you to learn more about the disciples' lives and the demands facing them, but it also models commitment. Visiting teenagers outside of the church walls takes special effort, signaling that you care.

3. *Invite teenagers to be on mission with God.* Make sure they understand they are not merely involving themselves in another church activity or event. Communicate the significance of what you are asking them to do. Make them aware that they are joining God in His mission on this earth—to bring all people to Himself. Such a cause requires more than casual commitment. Such awareness should make the student less inclined to offer excuses for abandoning the task.

4. *Reveal the Father.* Just as Jesus set the example for you by revealing the Father to His disciples, you can reveal the Father to those you disciple. Demonstrate in your life such Christlike characteristics as steadfastness and dependability. As you show that you can be relied on, they will see Christ in you. Ideally, they will understand that commitment is not just a rule but the very essence of who you are and who the Father is. God is committed to us; we need to make the same commitment to Him.

5. *Give assignments.* Watch closely how the disciples follow through. Praise them for sticking to a task and for not allowing other demands to weaken their commitment to Christ. If they fall short of the mark, try to determine what deterred them. Was it circumstances beyond their control, or was it a matter of attitude?

6. *Explain the requirements of a continuing relationship.* The Scriptures tell of temptation, trials, and suffering for those who follow Christ's commands. Living as a committed disciple does not protect us from Satan. In fact, it makes Satan want even more to ensnare you. Commitment to Christ in a personal, lifelong obedient relationship leaves us constantly on call. But no greater peace can be found than exists in a person who lives at the center of God's will and who follows Him every second of every day.

7. *Call for a deeper commitment.* Tell disciples they will be required to commit themselves far beyond anything they have ever experienced. Their prayer life, their time in the Word, their need to fellowship with others, the commitment to witness and serve will all be stretched to the maximum as they fully follow Christ. The rewards are a closer relationship with Christ and peace that results from living in His will.

THE IMPORTANCE OF MODELING

The most important way to lead teenagers in their relationships with Christ is to model the kind of relationship you want them to develop. You cannot teach what you are not practicing any more than you can come back from where you have never been. The heart of discipleship is living Christ's commands and then teaching them.

Obedience is the common denominator among the disciples Jesus called. Jesus chose persons who did not have many credentials. But they did what He said. They followed because they heard the Lord and obeyed Him. Although many times He asked them to do illogical things, they did them anyway. Do you want Jesus to reveal Himself to you? Then keep His commandments. *John 14:21* says: *"Whoever has my commands and obeys them, he is the one who loves me. He who loves me will be loved by my Father, and I too will love him and show myself to him."*

If you lead *MasterLife, Student Edition,* you must be obedient. Do not ask anyone to do something unless you have done it first. Regularly in "Before the Session" instructions for group sessions, you will be reminded to complete an assignment before the session so that you can share your experience as you train participants. If you do not practice what you preach, you make proselytes rather than disciples. Proselytes are sterile; they do not reproduce. To make reproducing disciples, do the things you say. Disciples will learn the things they see you do.

This modeling sequence will be valuable to you in your leadership style.

1. I do it whether or not anyone knows it.
2. I do it, and you observe.
3. You do it, and I observe you.
4. You do it and report.
5. You begin doing it whether or not anyone knows it.

LEADING DISCIPLES TO EXPERIENCE TRUTH

How do you lead a person to master a truth? As you just read, modeling plays a key role. The disciple respects you and is therefore willing to try an idea because he or she has seen you live it. However, a new disciple needs time to assimilate the scores of ideas he or she confronts. A disciple makes a truth a part of his or her life by practice. Here are five steps a disciple experiences in mastering a truth.

1. *Imitation.* You do what the model does. You may not understand the actions, but you do what you see the model doing.

2. *Experimentation.* You try out the truth in real life on your own. You believe it enough to experiment but are still not convinced. You begin trying it in nonthreatening situations.

3. *Application.* You apply the truth in more complex situations.

You say you believe the truth, but you may still have occasional reservations about it.

4. *Demonstration.* You show proficiency in living the truth under various conditions and situations. It has become a conviction and is part of your value system.

5. *Representation.* You model the truth as a characteristic of the life of a disciple.

Jesus used five principles in developing disciples toward the ideal of Christlikeness.

• *Modeling.* Doing something you cannot visualize is difficult. Once you have seen it modeled, forces in your personality combine to help you *imitate* it.

• *Explaining.* Modeling does not stand alone. It needs explanation. Jesus often explained the things He modeled so that His disciples would not misunderstand. The disciples responded by *experimenting.*

• *Coaching.* The discipler guides the disciple to do something more skillfully until the disciple becomes comfortable with the new way of doing things. This helps the disciple *apply* what he or she has learned.

• *Supporting.* The discipler supports the student in living the truth after he or she has mastered it. As disciples begin to live their new lifestyles and *demonstrate* what they have learned, they feel supported by someone more experienced.

• *Commissioning.* The discipler validates the disciples' ministries and sends them out with specific tasks to do. Jesus' urging of Peter to *"feed my sheep"* (see *John 21:15-18*) is an example of how Jesus used this principle to help His disciples *represent* Him in the world.

Let's look more deeply into the way Jesus used the principle of coaching to help disciples learn to practice a truth. Jesus taught truths again and again by various means that involved all the senses. He did not merely toss out a concept and hope it was caught. He repeated truths, modeled them, and guided the disciples while they applied them. If you are to help others transform their character into Christlikeness, they need to practice a truth until it becomes their own—as you guide them from the sidelines.

Jesus gave His disciples assignments and expected them to do them. Sometimes they failed, and Jesus stepped in to help them. In *Mark 9:29* when the disciples failed to drive out evil spirits, Jesus cautioned that only through prayer can such things occur. In *Matthew 17:14-20* Jesus told the disciples that their lack of faith prevented them from healing the epileptic boy. A wise coach knows when to let persons learn on their own and when to intervene.

CORRECTING DISCIPLES

Jesus did not limit Himself to merely positive relationships with His disciples. Jesus' disciples knew that He loved them, that He was concerned for their growth, and that He had great plans for their futures. But Jesus didn't develop them by giving only positive reinforcement when they did things right.

In the Book of Matthew alone are numerous examples of Jesus' correcting His disciples. For example, in *Matthew 8:23-26* when Jesus calmed the storm, He spoke sternly to the disciples about their lack of faith. In *Matthew 15:15-20* Jesus upbraided the disciples for their dullness in failing to understand the parable about eating with unwashed hands. In *Matthew 19:14* Jesus corrected the disciples for hindering the children from coming to Him.

Disciplers cannot sit idly by and allow those they disciple to err in belief or practice. Just because some persons abuse and misuse the concept of correction, we should not fail to correct for someone's benefit. Allowing disciples to continue in sin prevents their developing Christlike character and Kingdom values. If someone is to be on mission with God in the home, the church, and the world, he or she must be a good representative of Christ without having his or her witness tarnished by wrong actions or doctrines.

Here are suggestions on how to correct those you disciple.
1. Begin with positive statements.
2. State your concern and why.
3. Ask for the person's view of the problem.
4. Ask for possible solution(s).
5. Agree on a course of action.
6. Set a time for a follow-up meeting.

HOW TO LEAD A SMALL GROUP

Leading a small group can be exciting and rewarding. Your involvement with group members and in the group process can be a learning experience.

Understand Your Role as Leader

As the leader of a small group, you need information or skills in at least five areas: (1) knowledge of the work, (2) knowledge of responsibilities, (3) skill in instructing, (4) skill in improving methods, and (5) skill in leading.[1]

As you prepare to lead, ask yourself these questions.
• How can I get the group to accomplish its goals?
• How do I help the group grow and learn?
• How do I involve group members in meaningful activities?

Leading a group is not just relating information to a gathered audience. Encourage students to participate and share.

Your role as leader is not to bring glory to yourself. The best group learning usually takes place when the leader blends into the group and is not set apart. Read the following guidelines and consider what effect they would have on you and your small group.

• *Atmosphere.* Create an atmosphere that encourages each member to share ideas and invest talents. Convey acceptance to group members. This frees them to become involved and participate openly.

• *Goals.* Help move the group toward its established goals. Keep the group united and focused on its task.

• *Ministry.* Relate to the group in a servant capacity. Consider Jesus' role as leader and think about ways you can serve group members.

• *Criticism.* A mature leader who has created an accepting group atmosphere can allow room for healthy criticism and can cope adequately with hostility.

• *Feelings.* Participate as a group member and share your positive and negative feelings. Although you are the leader, you have a right to express your feelings as any other member would. Use nonthreatening "I feel" messages rather than accusatory "you" messages.

• *Failures.* Overcome your personal leadership mistakes and help group members overcome their failures. Inevitably, periods of discouragement, lack of interest, or low morale come. Learn from those times and move toward growth.

• *Total effort.* Concern yourself about the total group effort. Know what's happening within the group and encourage growth.

• *Acceptance.* Express your acceptance of group members. Listen to them, set aside your biases while they speak, and convey the fact that you consider them a significant part of the group. This signals that you expect them to contribute to the group and give their best. Be patient and allow them to share when they are ready. Put their needs ahead of your own.[2]

Arrange the Room for Learning

Use the following ideas to make the room arrangement and physical environment aid the group process.

• Arrange chairs in a circle or a semicircle so students can see one another face-to-face. Keep chairs relatively close together. Members communicate with their facial expressions or their body postures as much as they do with their comments.

• Remove any unnecessary items in the room. This is especially important if you are meeting at church. A room that is free of clutter, outdated materials, or excess equipment will enhance the learning process.

• Position training equipment, such as chalkboards, TV, posters, etc., so that all students can see without difficulty.

• Try not to place chairs facing a large window. Place chairs so the entrance is at the back of the room so latecomers can enter without embarrassment.[3]

Use Learning Methods That Involve Members

Your role is not the traditional teacher-pupil role in which the teacher is expected to have all the answers. Rather, your role as leader is that of a helper or a guide. Help the group discover problems and questions, find answers and solutions, and organize facts and information. Because these techniques are built into the procedures in this Leader Guide for each group session and workshop, it is best that you follow these instructions rather than design your own procedures.

Help Group Members Determine Their Roles

Model various helping roles within the group and encourage students to use roles that fit them. These roles encourage the hesitant member, keep a check on the dominating member, and keep the group on track. When your group seems to face problems with process, lead a discussion of the following roles. Help students identify who in your group plays which role.

• *Summarizer*—pulls together information that has been presented.

• *Mediator*—steps in and mediates when disagreement or tension occurs by pointing out benefits of both sides.

• *Decentralizer*—directs attention to others when several persons dominate the discussion. This person may say, "Mary, will you tell Tom about the time…?"

• *Initiator*—introduces a beginning point for the group when members have trouble getting started.

• *Information giver*—presents necessary information to the group.

• *Information seeker*—prevents the group from jumping to conclusions and steps in to say, "I think we need more facts."

• *Prober*—says, "Why do you say that? What do you mean by that?" when the students may not be getting to the heart of the matter.

• *Relaxer*—says, "Let me tell you a story about …" to provide time for ideas to gel or tempers to cool.

• *Encourager*—says, "You made a great point, and you are doing good work" when individuals contribute to the group and to the accomplishment of group goals.

• *Navigator*—brings the group back to the original purpose when members get off track.

• *Orienter*—deals with latecomers by saying, "Before you came in, we said…"

• *Evaluator*—reminds the group of how much it is accomplishing by saying, "We've already achieved two of our goals."

• *Clarifier*—steers through confusion or misunderstanding by restating information or by saying, "I believe what Mary Ann meant was …"[4]

As group members use these helping roles, they join the leader in assuming responsibility for group direction. They help everyone participate in a responsible, creative way.

HOW A *MASTERLIFE* SESSION WORKS

MasterLife, Student Edition, may be used in two different plans: the Standard Plan and the One-to-One or Mentoring Plan.

The Standard Plan is recommended. The One-to-One or Mentoring Study Plan may be used to lead an individual through *MasterLife, Student Edition*. It can also be used to help group members make up group sessions they have missed. Choose the plan that best meets discipleship needs.

The Standard Plan
1. Each group session is designed for 1 1/2 hours in length. Time increments are provided.

2. Students complete all weekly assignments before the group session.

3. Part 1—at each session students deal with the preceding week's assignments by discussing them, practicing skills learned, and checking to see that all assignments have been completed.
Part 2—each session also prepares students for the following week by giving additional training that will be incorporated into the coming week's assignments.

4. The leader uses the Leader Guide as directed. The first half of the session deals with material in part 1; the second half involves part 2.

The One-to-One or Mentoring Study Plan
1. The purpose of this plan is to...
   • meet discipleship needs when a *MasterLife, Student Edition* group is not feasible or when a special relationship lends itself to this approach. Examples are a parent and child, youth minister and youth leader, youth minister and student, youth leader and student, a person who needs considerable individual help, or a person who is experienced in discipleship training and wants to move at a faster pace so that he or she can use *MasterLife, Student Edition* to disciple others.

2. In this plan the student uses the basic outline for the Standard Plan. The leader studies the material and adapts it to the individual's needs and to the relationship. Each session in this Leader Guide suggests ways to do this under the heading "One-to-One or Mentoring Study Plan."

3. The time required for a session will vary according to the individual's needs. A one-to-one setting usually requires less time than a group setting. Use any extra time to deal with specific needs that arise.

4. Plan to meet at a specific time each week to work together. A regular meeting time is as important to one-to-one study as it is to group study.

A KEY DECISION
MasterLife, Student Edition, was written with the assumption that members have already received Jesus Christ as their Savior and Lord. However, sometimes *MasterLife* participants begin to realize as they study that they have never invited Christ into their lives. Be alert to this possibility. Guidance on how to receive Christ appears in each student book. Be available to answer questions for members who accept Christ when they reach these points in the study. Arrange for them to talk to a pastor or a church leader. Give them copies of *Truths That Make a Difference* and *Survival Kit for Youth, Revised*. These students may continue in *MasterLife, Student Edition*, but may also want to use *Survival Kit* as reference material.

AWARDING DIPLOMAS
A Christian Growth Study Plan and diploma may be awarded to a student who completes *MasterLife, Student Edition*. Eligibility requirements and application instructions appear at the end of the student book. Plan to award diplomas during a worship service or at another appropriate time when the church family can affirm participants.

OPTIONAL LEADER TRAINING
The following material provides a plan churches can use to train *MasterLife* group leaders. This training plan is optional. Special training is not necessary or required to lead *MasterLife, Student Edition* groups effectively. Group leaders can be equipped for their tasks by studying the student books, by studying the material in this Introduction, and by following the plan in this Leader Guide for each group session.

1. The leader of the following training sessions should be someone who has experienced *MasterLife*. That way the leader can give the presentations and can talk with more knowledge about the assignments and skills.

2. The following schedule will benefit you if you are ...
   • a leader of a *MasterLife* group who wants an overview of the entire process before you begin;
   • a *MasterLife* graduate who wants to lead a group and needs training;
   • church leaders beginning several *MasterLife, Student Edition* groups at the same time and need to train leaders.

3. After leaders train and while studies are in progress, leaders could meet regularly to debrief or solve problems.

4. *MasterLife* Training 1 is the training that should be offered before leading group sessions for *MasterLife, Student Edition.*

MasterLife Training 1 (5 1/2 hours)

Purpose: To equip *MasterLife* group leaders to lead *MasterLife, Student Edition* groups. After this training, prospective *MasterLife* leaders will be able to (1) describe the *MasterLife* process; (2) state the goal of discipling by writing the definition of discipleship; (3) list and define the six disciplines of the Disciple's Cross; (4) describe the origin and purpose of *MasterLife;* (5) affirm the importance of the leader's modeling the desired behavior; (6) explain the small-group practices used in *MasterLife, Student Edition.*

Preparation Checklist

❑ Schedule *MasterLife* Training 1. The schedule is listed for a Friday-night-and-Saturday time frame, but you can conduct the training any time you can schedule the two sessions.

❑ Enlist *MasterLife* leaders and explain the *MasterLife, Student Edition* study using the material in this Introduction.

❑ Provide Leader Guides for leaders to enable them to study the materials. You may want to view the optional adult *MasterLife* study video presentations when convenient. Some church members may want to supply these guides, or the *MasterLife* fee could include this cost.

❑ Assign the Introduction and Week 1 in *MasterLife, Student Edition* to be completed before the training.

❑ Determine a training site and make arrangements.

❑ Prepare the meeting room.

• Provide tables with groups of up to eight persons at a table to function as a *MasterLife* group.

• Provide comfortable chairs.

• Provide an overhead projector and screen or a chalkboard.

• Provide a VCR and a monitor.

• Provide extra paper and pencils for participants.

• Prepare refreshments for breaks.

• If possible, enlist facilitators who have already experienced *MasterLife* to lead small groups during the training.

Friday Night (3 hours)
1. Introduction (20 minutes)
• Ask members to introduce themselves to one another if they are not well acquainted. Have each person tell one fact that will help others remember his or her name.
• Describe the plans for the *MasterLife, Student Edition* studies in your church.

2. Purpose of *MasterLife, Student Edition* (30 minutes)
• Lead a group discussion of the why, what, who, where, when, and how of discipleship.

3. Small-group discussion (15 minutes)
• Have each participant state why he or she will lead a *MasterLife, Student Edition* group.
• Ask, **What difficulties do you anticipate?**

4. Break (20 minutes)

5. Overview "How Discipling Takes Place" (30 minutes)
• Ask participants to watch for the "Crowd," "Group," "Core," and "Individual" audiences in the discipling process and to identify which audience they are in as you overview the information under "How Discipling Takes Place," (p. 9).

6. Conversational prayer (20 minutes)
• Give instructions for conversational prayer on pages 132-133 of *MasterLife, Student Edition.* (5 minutes)
• Lead the group in conversational prayer. (15 minutes)

7. Overview the contents of the Leader Guide. Describe the *MasterLife* process. (35 minutes)
• Give the definition of discipleship on page 5 of this Leader Guide and discuss the elements of the definition. (10 minutes)
• Give a presentation of "The Disciple's Cross." (20 minutes)

8. Closure (10 minutes)
• Overview the schedule for tomorrow. Ask participants to bring their Leader Guides.
• Dismiss with a closing prayer.

Saturday Morning (2 1/2 hours)
1. Opening (5 minutes)
• Open with a familiar hymn or chorus. Call on someone to lead in prayer.

2. Experience Group Session 1 in *MasterLife, Student Edition.* (1 hour)

• Lead the session if you have fewer than eight people, carefully following the directions in this Leader Guide for session 1. If you have more than eight, divide the group and ask other facilitators to lead each small group.

3. Break (15 minutes)

4. Overview Student Resource (15 minutes)
   • Overview MasterLife, Student Edition

5. How to Enlist (10 minutes)
   • Discuss "How to Select Students to Disciple" and "Enlisting Disciples" on page 9 in this Leader Guide.

6. How to Lead a Small Group (15 minutes)
   • Briefly overview the information "How to Lead a Small Group" on page 13. Help them understand their role as leader in five areas.

7. The Leader as Model (15 minutes)
   • Overview material beginning on page 10, "The Importance of Modeling."

8. Roman Road (8 minutes)
   • Describe the evangelism training (p. 83-87) in the student book, learning the Roman Road gospel presentation, and writing their personal testimonies.

9. Closure (7 minutes)
   • Announce the schedule for leader training before the workshop at the end of each course. This will enable leaders to prepare for the workshop and be ready to lead the next study.
   • Discuss whether the leaders would like to get together with you for a check-up time at regular intervals during each study.
   • Join hands and pray conversationally for the MasterLife groups that are scheduled to begin.

MasterLife Training 2 (2 1/2 hours)
(Conduct before the Growing Disciples Workshop.)
Purpose: To equip MasterLife leaders to lead the Growing Disciples Workshop and weeks 7-12 of MasterLife, Student Edition.

1. Growing Disciples Workshop (35 minutes)
   • Review the purpose and schedule for the Growing Disciples Workshop, page 54-59.

• Ask the leaders to complete the Discipleship Inventory on page 207 of MasterLife, Student Edition and score it before they attend this workshop. Scoring instructions are on page 57 of this Leader Guide.
• Lead them through the inventory-debriefing.

2. Break (15 minutes)

3. Give the presentation of The Disciple's Personality yourself. (30 minutes)

4. Preview MasterLife, Student Edition, weeks 7-12 (30 minutes)
   • Show how the Disciple's Personality is learned one part at a time over a six-week period.
   • Call attention to the process for writing a salvation testimony on page 184 of MasterLife, Student Edition.

5. Personal-testimony Evaluations (20 minutes)
   • Give instructions for evaluating another person's testimony (Leader Guide, p. 77).

6. Preparing for the Testimony Workshop (5 minutes)
   • Show the agenda on page 97 in this Leader Guide.
   • Explain about enlisting persons to listen to testimonies.

7. In the Carpenter's Shop (10 minutes)
   • Explain that God is always shaping our character to match the assignment He has for us.
   • Show how "In the Carpenter's Shop" throughout weeks 7-12 gives direction and freedom for students to work on specific character traits.

8. Close with prayer for the Growing Disciples Workshop and for the future growth of MasterLife students. (5 minutes)

MasterLife Training 3 (1 hour)
(Conduct before the Testimony Workshop.)
Purpose: To equip MasterLife leaders to lead the Testimony Workshop.

1. Begin with prayer (5 minutes)

2. Ask leaders to share any concerns or questions they have about the Testimony Workshop. (15 minutes)

3. The Spiritual Armor (20 minutes)
   • Give the presentation in a conversational, testimony

mode, illustrating how you use each part of the armor in your personal prayer life.

4. Discuss the personal prayer journal that each participant will develop. (15 minutes)

5. Close the session by asking leaders to pray in groups of two or three. (5 minutes)

[1] LeRoy Ford, *Developing Skills for Church Leaders* (Nashville: Convention Press, 1968), 25.
[2] Stanley J. Watson, "How Groups Learn" *Skill,* July, August, September 1973, 115.
[3] Ford, 21.
[4] Ibid.

MASTERLIFE
STUDENT EDITION
LEADER GUIDE

"I am the vine; you are the branches.
If a man remains in me and I in him, he will bear much fruit;
apart from me you can do nothing" (John 15:5).

In *MasterLife, Student Edition,* weeks 1-6, God will use The Disciple's Cross
to lead students to develop a deeper relationship with Christ
as they practice the six biblical disciplines of a disciple.

Contents—Introductory Session and Weeks 1-6

INTRODUCTORY SESSION

How to Master Life

Conduct this Introductory Session before your group members study week 1 of *MasterLife, Student Edition*.

Session Goals
By the end of this session, youth will be able to demonstrate their commitment to *MasterLife* by…
- telling at least one new fact about each member;
- explaining the meaning of "abiding in Christ";
- saying from memory *Luke 9:23*;
- explaining the Disciple's Cross diagram;
- doing the assignments for week 1.

Standard Plan

BEFORE THE SESSION

❏ Secure copies of *MasterLife, Student Edition* for members.

❏ Review the Introduction; complete the learning activities for week 1 of *MasterLife, Student Edition*, to stay ahead of the group.

❏ In a quiet place pray for group members by name. Ask God to give you the wisdom you need to prepare for and lead the Introductory Session.

❏ Read "During the Session."

❏ Check with the host and/or hostess to be sure he or she is prepared for the group this week.

❏ Arrange for refreshments to be served at the beginning of the session.

❏ Arrange in a circle only enough chairs for everyone attending.

❏ Secure enough name tags for those you expect to attend.

❏ Have pens or pencils and extra blank paper on hand for the session.

❏ (**Note:** A video has been prepared for use with the adult *MasterLife* study material. You may want to view the video and use it with your student *MasterLife, Student Edition*, study group.) Choose either to show the video presentation of the Disciple's Cross or prepare to make the presentation yourself. If you decide to use the video, carefully preview it ahead of time, keeping in mind the needs of your youth using only those parts that will be most helpful in your situation. On page 102 is an overhead cel master of The Disciple's Cross that you may want to prepare and use for review each week.

❏ Secure video equipment and cue the tape before the session begins if you have decided to show the adult *MasterLife* video.

❏ Have on hand a chalkboard or newsprint/poster paper on which to draw the Disciple's Cross. You will draw the cross as you give the presentation.

❏ Enlist one person to help you lead phase 2 of the "Abiding in Christ" Bible study.

❏ Plan to stay within the times given for each activity. The maximum time suggested for each week is 45 minutes for each part. Because it is an introduction, times for this week's session are 35 to 50 minutes for each part. You may want to print an agenda each week with the subjects and times listed. This will guide the group and allow students to help the group stay on schedule.

Allowing students to share freely is far more important than sticking legalistically to a plan you develop for the group session. Group members sometimes arrive at a session eager to tell about something that happened in their lives during the week related to that week's content. Be sensitive to this need, and be flexible. Allow God to work in your group. Provide opportunities for everyone to respond during the session.

DURING THE SESSION
Part 1 (35/50 minutes)

Introduction (10/15 minutes)
1. Welcome each student and point them to the refreshments. Invite each person to make a name tag. As students arrive, introduce each one to the others in the room if they don't already know each other. Let everyone visit informally until time to begin.

2. Begin promptly. Remind the group that you will begin and end each session on time. If students want to fellowship or have additional discussions after the sessions, they may do so, but they can count on you to be prompt.

3. Use the following icebreaker: Ask each person to give his or her first name and tell the group two things about it.
   • Why did your parents give you this name?
   • How do you like your name?

Volunteer to begin. If you answer the questions in about 45 seconds, most of the students will also.

Autobiography Worksheet (35/45 minutes).
4. Give a copy of *MasterLife, Student Edition* to each member.

5. Ask students to complete the Autobiography Worksheet on page 8 of the student book. Discuss each question. Allow about 10 minutes for each one. Let students answer voluntarily. Demonstrate love and affirmation as you build understanding among group members.

Take a stand-up break. Invite students to help themselves to refreshments.

Part 2 (35/50 minutes)

Bible Study: "Abiding in Christ" (20/25 minutes)
1. Ask members to complete the Bible study "Abiding in Christ" individually (student book, p. 7). Explain that the Bible study will be divided into three periods: one-to-one, small group, and total group.

2. One-to-one: Ask students to pair up for five minutes to discuss their answers to phase 1 of the Bible study "Abiding in Christ." Ask members to share why they chose each answer.

3. Small groups: Ask two pairs to get together to discuss phase 2 of the Bible study. Instruct an extra pair to join a group of four or split them between the two groups. You as leader can lead one group; the person enlisted to help you can lead the second group. Encourage students to tell why they chose a particular answer.

4. Total group: Discuss phase 3 of "Abiding in Christ."

5. Introduce *Luke 9:23* and ask students to spend five minutes memorizing it. Explain this is the first of 13 verses they will memorize during *MasterLife, Student Edition*. Quote the verse yourself and teach them how to memorize using the following instructions.
   - Quote the first phrase, *"Luke 9:23: If anyone would come after me..."*
   - Quote the first and second phrases, *"Luke 9:23: If anyone would come after me, he must deny himself..."* Repeat this three times.
   - Quote the same and add the next phrase, *"and take up his cross daily."* Repeat all phrases three times.
   - Quote the total verse and ask volunteers to repeat it all. After three or four students have quoted it, ask members to say it to each other.

6. Say, **You have memorized the verse, but you will need to repeat it each day for a week (usually several times) and at least once each week during group time to put it into your long-term memory.**

7. Encourage students to vary the way they repeat the verse:
   - as a group
   - to themselves
   - to the person beside them
   - in writing
   - with one person starting and another person finishing it

The Disciple's Cross (10/20 minutes)
8. Use the Disciple's Cross presentation on pages 202–204 in the student book to model how the Disciple's Cross should be used. **Optional:** Instead of making the presentation yourself, you might want to use the adult study *MasterLife* video. Introduce the presentation by explaining that students will learn to give it just as you do. Ask them to take careful notes.

9. If you choose to give the presentation, do not read it. Illustrate it by drawing the cross on the chalkboard or on newsprint/poster paper. Students will learn to present it as you do; set a good example.

10. Do not call attention to the Disciple's Cross presentation in the student book until you have completed your presentation. If students discover it, ask them not to read it until the session is over.

11. Explain that you will be happy to help them as they develop in discipleship by spending time with the Master, living in the Word, praying in faith, fellowshipping with believers, witnessing to the world, and ministering to others. Say, **The Disciple's Cross will help you in several ways.**
   • **You will know the six disciplines of a disciple.**
   • **You will experience each of the six disciplines as it functions in your life each day.**
   • **You will be able to use them as the standard to remind yourself and to help other Christians see the commitments required for being Christ's disciple.**
   • **These disciplines will help you follow the direction of the Holy Spirit as you deal with problems in life.**
   • **You will be able to help other disciples live in Christ and bear fruit for His glory.**

Preview Week 1 Assignments (5/10 minutes)
12. Ask students to look at "My Walk with the Master This Week" for week 1 on page 10 of the student book. Review the specific assignments. Instruct them that as they complete an assignment, they will draw a vertical line through the diamond. A fellow student verifying their work during session 1 will draw a horizontal line through the diamond to form a cross.

13. Preview the content of week 1 briefly. Ask students to complete week 1, "Spend Time with the Master," before session 1. Tell them it will explain how they are to make Christ the center of their lives.

14. Call attention to the inventory at the end of week 1 (student book, p. 25). Ask students to complete the inventory before they attend session 1. Explain that the inventory is designed to show where each person is in his or her Christian life. Explain that it is not a test and is not designed to be shared with other people.

15. Use the chair diagram (Leader Guide, p. 5, overhead cel master p. 100) to illustrate the expectations for *MasterLife*. Call attention to the Discipleship Covenant on page 9 of the student book. Ask students to read it during the week and be prepared to sign it during next week's group session.

16. Tell students they will be asked to have a daily quiet time and to use the Daily Master Communication Guide in each day's material of week 1. Tell them that you will explain more about these two practices in next week's session.

Closure (5 minutes)

17. Announce the time and place for the next meeting.

18. Call attention to the suggestions about a prayer partner (student book, p. 10), and ask each person to enlist someone before the next session who is not in the *MasterLife* group.

19. Express gratitude that you are part of the group, and request students' prayers for you as you serve them during the weeks that follow.

20. Stand and join hands for a prayer of dismissal. Invite students to voice a one-sentence prayer. As leader, close the prayer time.

AFTER THE SESSION

❏ Before the next group session pray specifically for each member.

❏ Call and encourage each student in the study of the first week's material. Answer questions they may have, and encourage any who seem to need it. Thank each student for his or her participation.

❏ If any participants expressed doubt about joining the *MasterLife* group permanently, you may want to enlist others to take their place. Ask any new students to complete "Abiding in Christ" before the next session. They will be able to start week 1 with no problem. New members should not join the group after session 1.

❏ Use the following questions to evaluate your leadership.
  • Was I thoroughly prepared?
  • Was my presentation clear?
  • Did I follow the Leader Guide?
  • Did I provide positive leadership?
  • Was I a servant leader?
  • Did I create a group environment?
  • Did I help students communicate with each other?
  • Do students understand the purpose of the study?
  • Was I enthusiastic about how God will use *MasterLife* in students' lives and our church?

❏ Read "Before the Session" for the first group session to evaluate the amount of preparation you will need. At the top of the first page of Group Session 1 material, record when you will prepare.

❏ Carefully study week 2 and do all the exercises in the student book. You will preview week 2 for students during session 1.

One-to-One or Mentoring Study Plan

The activities for the Introductory Session will not take as long with one person as the times listed. You may want to shorten the session or go into greater detail by using the following additional instructions.

1. Share with the individual about persons, experiences, and events that have affected your values. Ask, **Where did you get your values? What effect did your home life have on them?** Discuss two or three significant events that have affected the person greatly.

2. Encourage the student by saying, **Talk about the needs you think *Master-Life, Student Edition* may help you meet. What previous experiences have helped you see the importance of discipleship training? What is your vision for your life?** As the leader, share your vision.

3. Ask, **What concerns you most about *MasterLife, Student Edition*? Discipline? Memorization? Pressures of other responsibilities? What concerns you about our discipling relationship?** As the leader, share concerns related to your leading a person through *MasterLife, Student Edition*.

GROUP SESSION 1

Spend Time with the Master

<table>
<tr><td>

Session Goals

By the end of this session, youth will be able to demonstrate their progress toward *MasterLife* goals by...
- sharing a sense of need after they complete the inventory at the end of week I;
- completing assignments for week I;
- explaining the center of the Disciple's Cross;
- telling their plans for a daily quiet time;
- asking group members to pray for a request.

</td></tr>
</table>

Standard Plan

BEFORE THE SESSION

❏ Review week I and read and complete the learning activities for week 2 of *MasterLife, Student Edition* to stay ahead of the group.

❏ Pray daily for each member of the group. Ask the Lord to give you the wisdom you need to prepare for and lead the group session.

❏ Master this week's material in the Leader Guide.

❏ Review the goals for this session.

❏ Check with the host or hostess about the plans for the group this week.

❏ Arrange the meeting place so that students can sit in a circle.

❏ Use name tags while students are still learning each other's names.

❏ Have pens or pencils and extra blank paper on hand for the session.

❏ Use a poster, chalkboard, or overhead cel (p. 101) of the following:
- Abide in Christ
- Obey Christ's Commands
- Learn by Doing
- Clarify Lessons Learned Through Experience
- Apply Lessons Learned

❏ Review the following instructions in preparation for the session.
- Do not be critical of students who do not memorize Scripture-memory verses word-perfect, but encourage them to work toward the mastery of each verse.
- Do not reprimand those who have problems completing assignments. Praise them for what they do; ask others to share any insights that might be helpful. Encourage members to bear each other's burdens.

DURING THE SESSION

Part I (45 minutes)

Introduction (10 minutes)

1. Greet students as they arrive. Begin on time. Be alert to any signs of progress

or any problems students may be facing. Open the session with prayer. Ask for special prayer requests.

2. Ask for volunteers to share how they felt when they completed the inventory (student book, p. 25). Do not ask for specific confessions; but if anyone would like to share their feelings, allow time for them to do so. Say, **As a group, all of you will need to help each other overcome obstacles to growth.**

3. Pair members to check each other's "My Walk with the Master This Week." Each person will ask the other person if he or she did the assignment and mark the diamond boxes accordingly. The student verifying may ask to see the work done. Students should quote memory verses correctly before this item is marked.

"Spend Time with the Master" (15 minutes)
4. Remind students that they are to complete the exercises and learn the material before they attend the group session. The reason for discussing the material in the group session is to reflect on it, explore the subject further, and apply it.

5. Ask, **Who is a disciple?** Allow volunteers to answer and surface any frustration they have in responding to this question. Take notes for future reference. Suggest that the students look for the answers to their questions as the group reviews this week's study.

6. Ask, **What were two reasons Jesus chose the disciples?** (See p. 12 in the student book; *to be with Him and to send them out.*)

7. Ask, **What did Jesus do when people began following Him?** (See p. 12 in the student book; *Jesus discouraged those who did not commit themselves fully to Him by first stating the requirements for being a disciple.*)

8. Ask students to open their Bibles to *Luke 14:26-33* and identify the three things over which Jesus said He must have priority. *(Persons, possessions, purposes.)*

9. Ask volunteers to share their answers to the activity about what presently may be taking priority over Christ in their lives (see p. 15 in the student book). If they do not respond readily, share your answer.

10. Ask someone to list the three characteristics Jesus says should be in a disciple's life. (See p. 17 in the student book; *obedience, love, fruit*).

11. Ask a volunteer to name two things that are required to obey Christ's commands today. (See p. 21 in the student book; *knowing them and doing them*).

12. Ask for volunteers to share their responses to the questions on pages 23-24 of the student book. Ask, **What would you do if Christ commanded you to do the things listed here?**

13. Ask, **As weak as most of us are, is it possible for us to obey and follow Christ?** Use *Philippians 2:13* and *John 15:5* to help students see that Christ provides us with the willingness and the ability to live the life of a disciple.

14. Ask youth to pray asking God to help group members make Christ the center of their lives.

How Jesus Made Disciples (10 minutes)

15. Use the poster or overhead cel you prepared before this session to explain how *MasterLife, Student Edition* uses some of the basic principles that Jesus used in making disciples. The following items in the session plan will guide you in your explanation. If you didn't prepare a poster, plan to write these items on a chalkboard.

16. *Abide in Christ.* Say, **This is our primary goal—to abide in Christ. The only way you can become true disciples is through the power Christ furnishes you to live the Christian life.** Ask students to examine the goals for this study on page 5 of their student books. After members have had time to review the goals, use the following questions to lead a discussion of how *Master-Life, Student Edition* will help them become better disciples. **What statements did you read that indicate this study will help you …**
… become a better disciple?
… become a more effective discipler?
… carry out the worldwide discipling task Christ has given you?

17. *Obey Christ's commands.* Say, ***MasterLife, Student Edition* is based on the fact that obedience to the lordship of Christ is the only way to learn to be a true disciple.**
   • Explain in your own words the information on the six biblical disciplines of *MasterLife* on page 5 of the student book.
   • Ask students to turn to page 10 for an example of the type of assignments they will have each week. Advise them to plan to spend 20 to 30 minutes each day to complete the assignments. Call attention to the fact that they will have an assignment in each of the six disciplines every week.
   • Explain that when a student completes an assignment, he or she should mark the diamond box in front of the assignment with a (vertical) line. At the next session, each student's assignments will be verified by another student, and the box will be marked by a horizontal line, forming a cross in each diamond.

18. *Learn by doing.* Say, **The assignments in "My Walk with the Master This Week" are based on the commands of Christ. They are modern applications of concepts and principles Jesus taught. They will help you obey Christ's commands and do His will. The most important learning will take place between sessions as you complete your assignments. Any assignment that is not completed will reduce the chances of learning.**

19. *Clarify lessons learned through experience.* Explain that at each group session they will spend time checking each other's assignments, reflecting on the past week's experiences, and practicing how to use their new skills and knowledge.

20. *Apply lessons learned.* Week by week students will be asked to apply the lessons they are learning to different situations. Each new application will be built on a previous lesson learned.

The Discipleship Covenant (5 minutes)

21. Ask students to turn to and read the covenant on page 9 of their student books. Although they may find some of the demands difficult now, encourage them to sign the covenant. Tell them that you and all the group members are covenanting to help each other keep these commitments. This is a commitment to try, with God's help and the help of the group and the leader. At this point you are looking for willing hearts. Explain that all are expected to sign the covenant. Invite questions. Then ask students to sign the covenants. Ask each student to pass his or her signed covenant to the right so each person can sign the covenant of every member in the group. Explain that praying for group members is an important part of *MasterLife*. Encourage them to refer to the list of students while they are learning names in order to pray for each other.

Take a short break. Invite youth to help themselves to refreshments.

Part 2 (45 minutes)

Group Prayer Time (5 minutes)

1. Ask students to mention specific prayer requests related to their daily quiet time or to their efforts to find prayer partners.

2. Invite members to pray short prayers. Tell them you will pray last. Lead in prayer after several have prayed. This period is not designed for a full-length prayer meeting.

Daily Quiet Time (10 minutes)

3. Share your personal plan for a daily quiet time. Do not mention the length of time unless someone asks you. You should emphasize the consistency more than the amount of time at this point. Note to members that they will learn more about the significance of their daily quiet times as they study the material in week 2 of their student books. Review the points in "How to Have a Quiet Time" on page 18 of the student book.

Prayer Covenant List (10 minutes)

4. Call attention to "How to Use the Prayer-Covenant List" on page 34 in week 2.

5. Explain how to use the Prayer-Covenant List on page 205 in the student book. Say, **You have permission to photocopy the Prayer-Covenant List. You may want to make individual lists for various categories of prayer or for different days of the week. Ideally, you will have at least one list of requests for which you pray daily. Other requests may be prayed for on a weekly or a monthly schedule.**

6. Say, **List each request in specific terms so you will know when it is answered. For example, do not write, "Bless Aunt Dolly." Instead, ask that Aunt Dolly might be able to use her arm again. Record the date requested. If the Holy Spirit impress on you a particular Bible verse related to that request, write that verse in the appropriate column.** (You may want to give a personal example.) **Be alert to verses in your Bible reading that might apply to your request. Later, we will study more about the different ways God answers prayer. Leave two or three lines on which to write entries in the answer column. Your prayer may be answered in stages. Write the date when each prayer is answered.**

7. Assure students that they are not expected to have enough prayer requests to fill all the lines. Suggest that they record only the requests that represent real concerns to them.

8. Tell students that they will be asked before session 2 to add at least five lost persons to their Prayer-Covenant Lists and to pray regularly for them.

9. Remind students that their prayer lists with dated answers may become the best evidence that they have to convince a skeptic of the concern and power of God.

10. Ask each student to share one request he or she has. Ask other members of the group to write that request on their Prayer-Covenant Lists.

Disciple's Cross Presentation (10 minutes)
11. Ask each student to pair with someone new to work with.

12. Instruct students to practice explaining and drawing for their partners the center of the Disciple's Cross and saying the verse that accompanies it. Both students will attempt to explain and draw the part of the cross they have learned. Remind them that they will add material each week to their presentation of the cross. By the end of this study they should be able to explain the Disciple's Cross in their own words.

Next Week's Assignments (5 minutes)
13. Ask students to look at "My Walk with the Master This Week" for week 2 on page 26 of the student book. Review the specific assignments. Make sure they understand how to complete each assignment.

14. Briefly preview the content of week 2. Ask students to complete week 2, "Live in the Word," before session 3. Tell them it will explain how they can grow closer to Christ as they learn to live in the Word by having a daily quiet time and memorizing Scripture.

15. Explain that they will be asked to get better acquainted with a member of the group during the next week. Remind them of the importance of this assignment so members can express support for each other.

Closure (5 minutes)
16. Announce the time and place for the next session.

17. Join hands in a prayer of dismissal. Ask students to say a one-sentence prayer thanking God for something that happened in today's session.

AFTER THE SESSION
❑ Evaluate the session by listing what you believe was effective. Consider ways to improve in future sessions.
❑ Make a Prayer-Covenant List for each student; record needs to be prayed for and answers to your prayers. Pray daily for each person (see *Phil. 1:6-8*).
❑ Contact anyone who needs encouragement or counsel. Be a servant who helps group members grow.
❑ Invite two students to visit or minister with you during the week. Do not ask them to do anything they are not experienced in doing. The purpose is for them to observe. Before each visit, tell them what you expect to find and do. After the visit, talk about why you conducted the visit as you did. Use the Roman Road gospel presentation (member book, pp. 84-87) when you witness each week so that students can be familiar with it before they are asked to learn it. This is one of the most important skills to teach by example.
❑ Read "Before the Session" for Group Session 2 to evaluate the amount of preparation you will need. At the top of the first page of Group Session 2 material, record when you will prepare.
❑ Carefully study week 3 and do all the exercises in the student book. You will preview week 3 for students during session 2.

One-to-One or Mentoring Study Plan

This session can be done by following the Standard Plan. Adapt the One-to-One or Mentoring Study Plan to the needs of the student. Future sessions require modification because of the group activities. Include the following options.

1. If you have extra time this week, give the student an opportunity to ask questions or to explore other areas he or she is interested in.

2. When discussing the inventory, go into more detail by asking the student to answer the questions at the conclusion of the inventory. Offer any help needed.

GROUP SESSION 2

Live in the Word

Session Goals

By the end of this session, students will be able to demonstrate their progress toward *MasterLife, Student Edition* goals by...

- giving and receiving support from group members on problems they may be having with weekly assignments;
- completing assignments for week 2;
- explaining the lower bar of the Disciple's Cross;
- making Prayer-Covenant Lists and praying for the requests of group members.

Standard Plan

BEFORE THE SESSION

❏ Review week 2 and read and complete the learning activities for week 3 of *MasterLife, Student Edition* to stay ahead of the group.

❏ Call group members and ask how they are doing with their assignments; encourage them in their work.

❏ Pray daily for each member of the group. Ask the Lord to give you wisdom to prepare for and lead the group session.

❏ Master this week's material in the Leader Guide.

❏ Review the goals for this session.

❏ Check with the host or hostess about their plans for the group this week.

❏ Arrange the meeting place so that students can sit in a circle.

❏ Have pens or pencils and extra blank paper on hand for the session.

DURING THE SESSION

Part I (45 minutes)

Introduction (25 minutes)

1. Begin the session on time even if all members are not present. The objective of this period is to allow students to share their progress and any problems they are having with *MasterLife*. Begin with prayer.

2. Ask several students to share one good experience related to completing their assignments this week. Limit this sharing to five minutes.

3. Take five minutes for students to identify any problem they may be having with any of the assignments. Ask members to suggest ways to solve these problems.

4. Ask students for reports on how they are doing with keeping a Prayer-Covenant List. Ask each student to volunteer one request that he or she put on

the list during the week. Invite students to pray a sentence prayer for the request of the person on his or her right.

5. Instruct youth to pair up and quote *John 8:31-32* to each other. While students work in pairs, they can check each other's "My Walk with the Master This Week" and draw the horizontal line in the student's diamond boxes after verifying completed work. Encourage the pairs to share their strong and weak points in completing the assignments.

"Live in the Word" (20 minutes)
Choose from the following items appropriate questions and activities for your group's study. Do not exceed the time allowance.

6. Ask, **Which of the four reasons given for having a quiet time is the most important to you? Why?** (The first listing of these four reasons is on p. 28 of the student book.) Ask them to suggest other reasons a quiet time is important.

7. Ask students to share benefits they see in a quiet time. Ask them to write the benefits in the margins of their workbooks as group members mention them.

8. Call for volunteers to tell how important a special time with God seemed to each of the following biblical characters: David, Daniel, John the Baptist, Jesus.

9. Ask, **How do you know a special time with God was important to the person just mentioned?** Say, **The reasons you gave are observable ways we can evaluate how important a personal time with God is to us.**

10. Ask students to write in the margins of their books these items: eating, fellowship with family, personal cleanliness, work, personal time with God. Ask them to rank them 1 (highest priority) through 5 (lowest priority). Then, ask, **What did you learn about yourself?**

11. Tell your experience of establishing a quiet time.

12. Ask a volunteer to share a time God helped him or her make a decision after seeking answers from His Word in a quiet time.

13. Ask a volunteer to tell what he or she would need to give up in order to establish a regular time of fellowship with God.

14. Remind students that before next week they will be asked to share with a friend their testimony of having a quiet time with someone who needs to develop this practice.

15. Ask students to pray with you. Voice a prayer asking God to help them make a daily quiet time a part of their lives.

Take a break and invite youth to help themselves to refreshments.

Part 2 (45 minutes)

Prayer Time (10 minutes)
1. Ask students to mention specific praises they have regarding their experiences in *MasterLife, Student Edition* so far.

2. Suggest that each member pray a short prayer of thanksgiving for the praise he or she just mentioned. Pray a brief prayer and invite volunteers to pray also.

The Disciple's Cross (25 minutes)
3. Form two small groups to practice presenting the Disciple's Cross. Two members of each small group will present the center circle of the Disciple's Cross. Two other members will present the lower bar of the Disciple's Cross. Other members of the group, if any, can indicate what points not covered in the presentation. Explain, **The purpose of this activity is to make sure each person has gained an understanding of the elements in the Disciple's Cross learned so far. Each of you is responsible for learning the presentation in your own words and having that presentation affirmed by another member of our group. You may move at your own pace, but each of you should master the complete Disciple's Cross presentation by the end of week 6.**

Next Week's Assignments (15 minutes)
4. Ask students to look at "My Walk with the Master This Week" for week 3 on page 42 of the student book. Review the specific assignments. Make sure they understand how to complete each one.

5. Preview the content of week 3 briefly. Ask students to complete week 3, "Pray in Faith," before session 3. Tell them it will explain how they can grow in their relationship with Christ through praying in faith.

6. Call attention to the assignment about showing God's love to a person who is not a Christian. Explain that members may decide for themselves how to show love to this person. Share any experiences you have in relating in this way to a person who is not a Christian.

7. Talk about opportunities to get together with students or take them with you as you witness or minister. Times together outside the regular meeting period can be the best for helping people grow as disciples.

Closure (5 minutes)
8. Announce the time and place for the next meeting.

9. Stand and join hands. Invite students to voice a one-sentence prayer for the

person on his or her right. Say, **Ask God to help this person grow in his or her relationship with God through** *MasterLife, Student Edition.*

AFTER THE SESSION

❏ Use the following questions to evaluate how well you led the session.
- Did everyone participate in the discussions?
- Did I affirm students for what they did well?
- Did I encourage those who are having a difficult time?
- Did the students understand my explanations?

❏ Talk individually with students who are not keeping up with the group.
- If they lack motivation, discuss reasons for their feelings.
- If they lack time, help them determine how to use time wisely.
- If they lack consistency, help them with self-discipline by showing them how to plan. Help them find a partner in the group who will check with them periodically.
- If they lack understanding, clarify the "how to" by doing the activity with them.

❏ Take a couple of students with you as you minister or witness.

❏ Ask one student to be your assistant. This person will assist in leading sessions and other group activities during the weeks ahead. Spend adequate time training this student to help you lead the group. This Leader Guide will give suggestions for involving this student in assisting you.

❏ Read "Before the Session" for Group Session 3. Evaluate the amount of preparation you will need for the next group session. At the top of the first page of session 3, record when you will prepare.

❏ Carefully study week 4 and do all the exercises in the student book. You will preview week 4 for students during session 4.

One-to-One or Mentoring Study Plan

Follow the instructions in the Standard Plan with the exception of asking the individual to respond to all questions. When discussing the quiet time, go into detail by asking the student to discuss particulars of his or her efforts at having a quiet time. Be prepared to share your experiences as well.

GROUP SESSION 3

Pray in Faith

Session Goals
By the end of this session, youth will be able to demonstrate their progress in achieving the *MasterLife* goals by...
- incorporating thanksgiving, praise, confession, and asking into their prayer time;
- completing week 3 assignments;
- explaining the upper bar of the Disciple's Cross;
- telling group members how they showed love to non-Christians;
- praying for their personal needs and the needs of others.

Standard Plan

BEFORE THE SESSION
❑ Review week 3 and read and complete the learning activities for week 4 of *MasterLife, Student Edition* to stay ahead of the group.
❑ Pray daily for each member of your group.
❑ Master this week's material in the Leader Guide.
❑ Review the goals for this session.
❑ Check with the host or hostess to be sure he or she is ready for the group this week.
❑ Arrange the meeting place so that students can sit in a circle.
❑ Have pens or pencils and extra blank paper on hand for the session.
❑ Use the MasterTime form and worksheet on page 206 in the student book to schedule your time and determine your priorities. Be able to share from your experience how this has helped you. Consider reading other material on time management.

Remember that allowing students to share freely is far more important than sticking legalistically to a plan you develop for the group session. Students sometimes arrive at a session eager to tell about something that happened in their lives during the week related to that week's content. Be sensitive to this need, and be flexible. Allow God to work in your group. Provide opportunities for everyone to respond during the session.

DURING THE SESSION
Part 1 (45 minutes)

Introduction (25 minutes)
1. Arrive early and fellowship with students as they arrive. Be alert and available to discuss any questions they may have. Begin on time.

2. Ask volunteers to share needs in their lives. Begin by sharing one of your own needs. If you are open and honest, it will set the stage and make it easier for others to share their needs.

3. Ask if anyone has an update on any prayer requests that group members have mentioned.

4. Lead the group to pray short prayers related to personal needs or the prayer requests mentioned.

5. Pair students and ask them to check each other's "My Walk with the Master This Week." They can use any extra time to review memory verses.

"Pray in Faith" (25 minutes)

Choose from the following list appropriate questions and activities for your group's study. Do not exceed the time allowance.

6. Invite a volunteer to share about an experience of praying on the basis of what he or she wanted rather than seeking God's will first (student book, p. 43). Tell your own experience in this area.

7. Call for volunteers to tell which of their Prayer-Covenant List requests they have seen answered.

8. Ask students why they believe thanksgiving and praising God occur first in prayer. Invite volunteers to share benefits they have experienced from coming before the Father with praise and thanksgiving first.

9. Ask, **Which name of God explained in day 3 has been most helpful to you in learning to praise Him?** Allow several members to respond.

10. Ask, **How do we distinguish between praising God and thanking Him?**

11. Ask, **Why do you believe confessing sin is important?** Invite a volunteer to share how he or she found that confessing sin helped restore a right relationship with God.

12. Invite a volunteer to tell about a time when he or she prayed with the wrong motivation or for an outcome that he or she later saw would not be Christ-honoring.

13. Invite several students to share one of the personal needs they listed in the student book on pages 56. Voice a prayer asking God to help group members with the specific requests mentioned.

14. Discuss why group members believe God wants them to intercede for oth-

ers. Ask each student to pray silently for someone on his or her Prayer-Covenant List.

15. Ask two or three volunteers to answer these questions: **Which of the four types of prayers is the easiest for you to pray? Which is most challenging? Why?**

Take a stand-up break. Invite students to help themselves to refreshments.

Part 2 (45 minutes)

Call to Prayer (5 minutes)
1. Invite the group to come back together. Ask members to describe their experiences this past week in showing God's love to a person who is not a Christian. Ask them to voice prayers for concerns others have mentioned regarding these non-Christian friends.

The Disciple's Cross (15 minutes)
2. Ask each student to pair with a person with whom he or she has not yet worked. Instruct each person to present to the other in his or her own words the material learned so far on the Disciple's Cross. Members have likely mastered the vertical bar and the center circle. Remind them that they may move at their own pace, but everyone is expected to master the complete Disciple's Cross presentation by the end of week 6.

MasterTime (15/20 minutes)
3. Say, **Some of you may find it difficult to add the MasterLife assignments to an already busy life. This training will help you learn to manage your time better and rethink your priorities. Setting goals and making long-range plans will enable you to do the most important tasks first.**

4. Briefly introduce "Redeeming the Time" on page 69 in the student book by summarizing the key thoughts.

5. Introduce the MasterTime form and worksheet on page 206 in the student book as a vehicle to help them set priorities and manage their time. Say, **To manage time is to manage life.**

6. Ask students to take notes as you explain how to use time wisely. You may refer to "How to Use MasterTime" (student book, pp. 72-73). Students will study the material later, but they should take notes now to help them learn. Explain each point, including the following:
   • *Trust the Lord.* Begin by listing the activities you will do as a part of walking with the Master for this time period.
   • *Plan your daily work.* Explain that they should use a few minutes at the begin-

ning or end of the day to plan their use of time for the next 24 hours.

- *Ask the Lord.* Encourage students to pray as they make their plans.
- *Depend on the Lord.* Give examples of how you deal with interruptions.
- *Discipline yourself.* Encourage students to master their time but not to become a slave of their planning. We are not trying to reduce spontaneity but to encourage the wise use of time.
- *Leave the results to God.* Tell students to work when they should but to leave for tomorrow tasks they cannot finish. Worrying or becoming a workaholic interferes with the best use of time.

Next Week's Assignments (5 minutes)

7. Ask members to look at "My Walk with the Master This Week" for week 4 (student book, p. 58) and preview the specific assignments. Make sure the students understand how to complete each assignment.

8. Briefly preview the content of week 4. Ask students to complete week 4, "Fellowship with Believers," before session 4. Tell them the material will explain how they can grow in their relationship with Christ through fellowship with believers.

9. Call attention to the assignment about getting to know someone in the church who is not a close friend or is not in the *MasterLife, Student Edition* study group. Give examples of how to get to know someone. Tell students they are to decide the best way to befriend the persons they choose.

Closure (5 minutes)

10. Offer individual help outside class if needed. Some members may feel overwhelmed by the amount of work or may feel stuck on an aspect of their work, such as Scripture memorization. Encourage them to contact you if they need help.

11. Answer any questions students may have. Close with prayer.

AFTER THE SESSION

❑ Use the following questions to evaluate how well you led the session.
- Do students care for each other? Are they trusting each other? Are they becoming more open with each other?
- Are there blocks in communication?
- Are students responding well to my leadership?
- Is the group becoming cliquish? Do I need to encourage members to keep reaching out?
- Do some students show undesirable attitudes toward other members? Should I take them visiting together and/or pair them up more often?
- Are students helping disciple each other?
- Do they see me as a growing disciple who also is learning from them?

❑ Continue to invite students to go witnessing and ministering with you. Take them on church visitation or hospital calls.

❑ Call or see all members of the group this week to encourage, enable, or challenge them as needed. Some will be struggling over how to manage time so they can complete their assignments. Remember that you are their servant. Involve your assistant in helping you.

❏ Read "Before the Session" for Group Session 4 to evaluate the amount of time you will need to prepare for the next group session. Record at the top of the first page of the Group Session 4 material when you will prepare.

❏ Carefully study week 5 and do all the exercises in the student book. You will preview week 5 for students during session 4.

One-to-One or Mentoring Study Plan

Follow instructions for the Standard Plan, with the following suggested variation. Give adequate time to help the person incorporate praying in faith into his or her life.

1. Help the student plan the next day's activities, using the MasterTime form and worksheet.

2. If the student is having difficulty understanding where he or she wastes time, ask them to keep a log of what he or she does for each 15-minute segment of time during the following week. This will be a time-consuming activity for the week, but it will reveal where time is being wasted and help the student plan to control it better in the future.

Fellowship with Believers

Session Goals

By the end of this session, students will be able to demonstrate their progress toward *MasterLife, Student Edition* goals by...
- sharing about their progress in having a quiet time;
- completing assignments for week 4;
- explaining the right crossbar of the Disciple's Cross;
- managing their time efficiently for the following week;
- sharing about their experiences in getting to know someone who is not in their immediate circle of friends.

Standard Plan

BEFORE THE SESSION

❏ Review this week's material and read and complete the learning activities for week 5 of *MasterLife, Student Edition* to stay ahead of the group.

❏ Pray daily for each member of your group.

❏ Master this week's material in the Leader Guide.

❏ Review the goals for this session.

❏ Check with the host or hostess to be sure he or she is ready for the group this week.

❏ Arrange the meeting place so that students can sit in a circle.

❏ Have pens or pencils and extra blank paper on hand for the session.

❏ Begin making plans for the Growing Disciples Workshop. Brief students on the plans at the close of this session. Prepare an overhead cel of the date, time, and place using the master on page 103. Make the following arrangements.

- *Meeting place.* Select a meeting site at the church or choose another adequate setting.

- *Time.* Three hours are recommended; 21/2 hours are the minimum. The workshop could be scheduled on a Saturday morning or Saturday afternoon, on a weeknight with an early meal preceding it, on a Sunday afternoon after a pizza party, or on two weeknights. Select the time most workable to your group members.

- *Food/refreshments.* Refreshments should be prepared for break. You might suggest that students bring favorite snacks for break time. If a meal is involved, suggestions include a meal served by the church, parents, or a local pizza delivery service if you are meeting on Saturday or Sunday.

- *Supplies.* Newsprint or large sheets of paper or a large chalkboard for drawing; extra pens or pencils, and paper.

- *Cost.* You may want to charge a fee to cover meals/snacks if students do not provide these.

❏ Prepare a copy of each of the following case studies for the Scripture-memory activity.

Case Study 1: Imagine that you are part of a group of Christians who have been put in jail. Your Bible has been taken from you. You want to reproduce the Bible word-perfect. How would you pool your knowledge to help each other memorize the Bible so you could remember the Word if you were later sent to separate cells?

Case Study 2: You are part of a group of teachers who work with students with learning disabilities. The students have average intelligence but find it difficult to read and remember. Nevertheless, they are eager to learn. What would you do to help them memorize Scripture?

Case Study 3: You are one of a group of teachers who work with underprivileged teenagers. These teenagers ride the church bus. They see no need for Scripture memorization. What could you do to convince them of the importance of Scripture memorization?

Case Study 4: You have moved to another city and joined a church. You have been asked to lead Scripture-memorization sessions for a group of teenagers in Discipleship Training. The members of the group give the usual excuses, such as:
- "I can't memorize."
- "I forget it as soon as I memorize it."
- "I've gotten along all right so far without Scripture memorization."
- "I don't have time."

What could you tell this group to help them make Scripture memorization a lifestyle?

❏ Review "How to Use MasterTime" on page 72 in the student book, and be prepared to answer any questions.
❏ Take a different person or persons visiting or ministering with you.

DURING THE SESSION
Part 1 (45 minutes)

Introduction (20 minutes)
1. Ask how many benefited from using MasterTime this week. Ask students to share ways they have been helped.

2. Ask students to share their problems with time management.

3. Give suggestions based on "How to Use MasterTime" (student book, p. 72) and "Redeeming the Time" (student book, p. 69). Encourage students to use time wisely by planning and letting the Master guide them.

4. Ask students to report how many times they had a quiet time during the week. Let each member share openly. Highlight that a place to mark each day was provided in "My Walk with the Master This Week" (student book, p. 58).

5. Praise God for progress students have made to this point. By now they should be able to have a quiet time at least five days of seven.

6. Ask students to share ways they have learned to overcome problems connected with setting aside a quiet time. Encourage them to support and help each other.

7. Pair students to check each other's "My Walk with the Master This Week."

"Fellowship with Believers" (25 minutes)
Choose from the following list appropriate questions and activities for your group's study. Do not exceed the time allowance.

8. Ask a volunteer to share about an experience of trying to go it alone as a Christian rather than staying connected to the fellowship of believers (see student book, p. 62). Share your experience in this area.

9. Ask, **Why is someone who professes to be a Christian, yet does not attend church, living outside God's will?** (Christ commands us to love each other and to encourage each other in the body of Christ. To do otherwise is disregarding God's Word.)

10. Ask, **Would someone tell about a time when you found it especially meaningful to fellowship with Christians?** Allow two or three students to respond.

11. Ask volunteers to share their answers to the case studies of Anita and Charles on page 63 of the student book. Ask, **Have any of you had an experience with befriending someone in need as these two case stories illustrate?** Encourage students to share circumstances, not names.

12. Invite youth to tell how they would answer a fellow believer who says, "I can worship God far better when I'm enjoying nature at leisure than I can in a church on Sunday morning." Ask students to share situations in their lives in which they struggled with issues about regular participation in the body of Christ.

13. Ask students to respond to the statement in the exercise on page 67 of the

student book:"Friends care enough to confront one another in love if necessary." Ask, **Do you believe that Christians can confront each other in a loving, Christ-honoring way? Would someone share about a time when they confronted another person this way?**

14. Ask, **What was the difference between the relationship of a servant and his master and the relationship the disciples had with Jesus?** (See p. 70, student book.) *(A servant would not know His Master's business. Jesus called the disciples friends.)*

15. Ask, **What were the three reasons Jesus gave for choosing His disciples?** (see p. 70, student book). *(To bear fruit, to ask the Father in His name, and to love one another.)*

16. Ask several volunteers to share about a time when they were witnessing and their fellowship with other believers supported them.

17. Invite each group member to pray silently that he or she will continue to see the difference that fellowship with other believers can make in living life in Christ.

Take a stand-up break. Invite students to help themselves to refreshments.

Part 2 (45 minutes)

Prayer Time (15 minutes)
1. Call the group together. Ask students to describe briefly their experiences this past week in getting to know someone who is not in their close circle of friends or in the *MasterLife* group. Emphasize that students do not need to give the names of the persons they got to know but merely describe circumstances. Ask group members to voice prayers for concerns others have mentioned regarding these situations.

The Disciple's Cross (5 minutes)
2. Ask each student to pair with a person with whom he or she has not yet worked. Instruct each person to present to the other in his or her own words the material learned so far on the Disciple's Cross. Students should have mastered the center circle, the vertical bar, and the right crossbar. Remind them that they will be able to explain the complete Disciple's Cross in their own words by the end of week 6.

Next Week's Assignments (20 minutes)
3. Focus the group's attention on "How to Memorize Scripture" (student book, p. 90). Ask students to remain in pairs. Have each pair discuss one of the case studies you prepared. Ask them to compile a one-minute report for the group. If you have more than four pairs, let extra people join a pair for this discussion.

4. Ask each pair to report on their case study and tell in about one minute how they would attempt to solve the problem. Ask students to take notes on helpful ideas they can use for Scripture memorization. After the reports ask each member to tell one idea he or she noted.

5. Ask students to turn to "Reasons to Memorize Scripture" on page 89 in the student book. Review the reasons for Scripture memorization and illustrate them from your personal experiences. Encourage them to read Bible references related to the reasons during the next week. Emphasize each practical suggestion that "How to Memorize Scripture" gives.

6. Preview other assignments for next week. Ask students to look at "My Walk with the Master This Week" for week 5, page 74, and preview the specific assignments. Make sure the students understand how to complete each assignment.

7. Preview the content of week 5 briefly. Ask students to complete week 5, "Witness to the World," before Group Session 5. Tell them it will help them bear witness to Christ and to their relationship with Him.

8. Announce plans for the Growing Disciples Workshop. Announce the time, date, and place. If you prepared an overhead cel, use it at this time. Discuss plans for food and snacks. Answer questions they might have. Make sure everyone understands that this workshop is not an optional activity but is a time to bring completion and experience celebration for all that members have accomplished. All assignments are to be completed before the workshop.

Closure (5 minutes)

9. Ask students to review "My Walk with the Master This Week" at the beginning of each week's study they have completed so far. Suggest that they have each item checked off as soon as possible to keep these activities from accumulating at the end of the book. Remind them that everyone needs to complete all items before the group moves on to weeks 7-12.

10. Announce next week's meeting place and time. Close with prayer.

AFTER THE SESSION

❑ Contact students who are having difficulty completing their assignments. Ask if you can do anything to help.

❑ Take two members with you to minister or to witness. Students will find it easier to minister or witness if they have been with someone else under these circumstances. As you witness, try to use the Roman Road gospel presentation described in week 5.

❑ Pray daily for all youth. Remember their prayer requests. Pray that they will be successful in hiding God's Word in their hearts.

❑ Continue to work on arrangements for the Growing Disciples Workshop, especially if you have decided to have the workshop away from your regular meeting site.

❑ Read "Before the Session" for Group Session 5 to evaluate the amount of time you will need to prepare for the next group session. At the beginning of session 5 material, record when you will prepare.

❑ Carefully study week 6 and do all the exercises in the student book. You will preview week 6 for students during session 5.

One-to-One or Mentoring Study Plan

Follow instructions for the Standard Plan. Select any of the following adjustments to make your one-to-one experience more effective.

1. Check your partner's time log. If you asked the student to make a time log, analyze it. Look for the following.
- Wasted time.
- Interruptions not dealt with appropriately.
- Lack of organization in doing tasks of a similar nature.
- Tasks that could have been delegated to others.
- Not gathering necessary materials before starting a task.
- Insufficient planning.
- How time totals for tasks compared with stated priorities.
- How to plan and utilize time better.

2. Review your partner's notes on the Daily Master Communication Guides for the week. If the student is having difficulty having a consistent quiet time, you may suggest calling each morning this week when you have your quiet time.

3. During the study, be frank about any battle you may have had in failing to draw spiritual nourishment from the fellowship of believers. Share suggestions you have found helpful in benefiting from your fellowship with God's people.

4. Present the material related to the left crossbar of the Disciple's Cross, and ask your student to note anything different from the presentation in *MasterLife*.

Witness to the World

Session Goals
By the end of this session, students will be able to demonstrate their progress in achieving the *MasterLife, Student Edition* goals by...
  • reporting on a new friend who is a non-Christian and praying for the non-Christian friends of others;
  • completing assignments for week 5;
  • explaining the left crossbar of the Disciple's Cross;
  • giving and receiving support on problems that arise with Scripture memorization.

Standard Plan

BEFORE THE SESSION

❑ Review week 5 and read and complete the learning activities for week 6 of *MasterLife, Student Edition* to stay ahead of the group.

❑ Pray daily for each member of your group.

❑ Master this week's material in the Leader Guide.

❑ Review the goals for this session.

❑ Check with the host or hostess to be sure he or she is ready for the group this week.

❑ Arrange the meeting place so that students can sit in a circle.

❑ Have pens or pencils and extra blank paper on hand for the session.

❑ Review "How to Memorize Scripture" (student book, pp. 90-91).

❑ Review daily all memory verses to date to be sure that you know them perfectly for the Scripture-memorization review at the upcoming Growing Disciples Workshop.

❑ Review final plans for the Growing Disciples Workshop so you can share them with group members.

DURING THE SESSION
Part 1 (45 minutes)

Introduction (20 minutes)
1. Ask students to share the names of non-Christian friends they made during the past week. Ask them to write all names on their Prayer-Covenant Lists as members share what they know about their new friends. Let each person share before you lead a time of prayer for all. If some students failed to make new friends, ask everyone to pray that God will lead these members to non-Christians they can befriend.

2. Pray for the lost friends who have been mentioned. Ask students to pray for

these people by name during the week. Read the promise in *Matthew 18:19.*

3. Ask, **How are you doing with your Scripture memorization? What problems are you having?** Share a challenge that you have had in this area. Review "How to Memorize Scripture" (student book, pp. 90-91). Encourage students to continue to work on this process and to pray for God's guidance.

4. Ask students to work in pairs to check each other's "My Walk with the Master This Week" and share an insight from the Daily Master Communication Guide.

"Witness to the World" (25 minutes)
Choose from the following list appropriate questions and activities for your group's study. Do not exceed the time allowance.

5. Ask, **Will a volunteer please share an experience of trying to rely on your own strength as you share Christ with other people rather than relying on the Holy Spirit to empower you?** Tell of your experience in this area.

6. Ask students why they believe that giving a verbal witness in addition to having Christlike traits in their lives is important.

7. Call for a volunteer to tell about a time when someone's comment about a positive trait seen in them provided an opportunity for a verbal witness.

8. Ask each student to choose one of the fruit of the Spirit mentioned in *Galatians 5:22-23* and tell how it can become the basis of a verbal witness (see student book, pp. 75-77).

9. Ask members to describe excuses they have made for not witnessing. Share one of the excuses you have made in the past.

10. Ask, **Will someone please tell about a time that Jesus worked so powerfully in your life that you could not help but tell what you had experienced?** Allow two or three students to respond.

11. Ask volunteers to share where they believe they are in their readiness to testify about what Christ has done in their lives.

12. Read aloud *John 15:20-21.* Ask students how they feel about the fact that bearing fruit for Christ has its price. Ask for a volunteer to share about a price he or she has paid for being a Christian.

13. Ask students to recall the types of suffering Jesus encountered other than the ones listed on page 88 in the student book. Remind them that Jesus was the only sinless person who has ever lived; His suffering was completely undeserved.

14. Close this part of the session by asking students to pray for the person on their right. Ask God to help this person bear fruit by learning to give a verbal witness for Christ.

Take a break. Invite students to help themselves to refreshments.

Part 2 (45 minutes)

The Disciple's Cross (20 minutes)

1. Ask students to get in pairs to check each other's presentation of the Disciple's Cross so far. Students likely will have mastered the center circle and the vertical and horizontal bars. Remind them that they will need to present the complete Disciple's Cross in their own words in next week's session so each person is signed off on this presentation before the Growing Disciples Workshop. In checking off the presentation, each person will be asked to quote all the verses that accompany the Disciple's Cross.

Next Week's Assignments (20 minutes)

2. Describe the upcoming Growing Disciples Workshop. Explain its purpose.

3. Ask students to look at "My Walk with the Master This Week" for week 6 on page 92 and preview the specific assignments. Make sure they understand how to complete each assignment. Urge them to complete all assignments before the Growing Disciples Workshop. At the workshop students will be asked to share with others what they have learned.

4. Briefly preview the content of week 6. Ask students to complete week 6, "Minister to Others," page 92, before session 6. Tell them it will help them minister to others as they learn to take up their crosses and follow Christ.

5. Call attention to the Discipleship Inventory on page 207 in the student book. Say, **The inventory is a way to evaluate your growth in discipleship. It is based on the characteristics of a disciple. You will score and interpret your responses at the Growing Disciples Workshop. Be as honest as possible in evaluating yourself. Wait until after session 6 and before the workshop to complete the inventory.**

6. Point out to students that before the Growing Disciples Workshop, they will be asked to draw something to illustrate the concepts of the Disciple's Cross. This learning activity will indicate how well they understand the truths illustrated in the Disciple's Cross. Urge them to draw the picture even if they don't believe they have artistic ability—concepts, not artwork is the important thing.

Closure (5 minutes)

7. Announce the time, date, and place for the Growing Disciples Workshop. Provide information about transportation to the site if the workshop is held away from your regular meeting place.

8. Close with prayer. Thank God for the progress students have made. Ask God for courage, wisdom, and efficient use of time in the week ahead to prepare for the Growing Disciples Workshop.

AFTER THE SESSION

❑ Pray for those who are struggling to keep up with the assignments. Pray that they will use their time wisely during the coming week to catch up in areas where they are behind.

❑ Ask God to guide students as they take the Discipleship Inventory. Ask Him to give them courage to be honest with their responses.

❑ Take two members with you to minister or to witness. Perhaps you can visit some of the persons on their Prayer-Covenant Lists.

❑ Make final arrangements for the Growing Disciples Workshop. Contact the meeting site to confirm arrangements for food, meeting space, and other matters. Arrange for any materials you need for the workshop.

❑ Send an invitation to each member listing the time, date, and place of the Growing Disciples Workshop (see sample below).

In acknowledgment of your walk with the Master
and to celebrate your completion of weeks 1-6 of
MasterLife, Student Edition,
you are cordially invited
to attend a
Growing Disciples Workshop.
(time • date • place)

*Please bring your book indicating your completed assignments
and your completed Discipleship Inventory.*

Enclose a map if the workshop will be held away from your regular meeting site. Furnish a phone number where students could be reached in an emergency. Provide other instructions if members are to bring a sack lunch or snacks.

❑ Read "Before the Session" for week 6 to evaluate the amount of time you will need to prepare for your next group session. At the top of the week 6 material record when you will prepare.

❑ Begin to preview weeks 7-12 of *MasterLife, Student Edition.* You will preview these chapters for members during the Growing Disciples Workshop.

One-to-One or Mentoring Study Plan

Follow instructions for the Standard Plan. Spend time on the Disciple's Cross by letting your partner give the presentation to you. Affirm his or her work and encourage further mastery of the material.

GROUP SESSION 6

Minister to Others

Session Goals

By the end of this session, students will be able to demonstrate their progress toward *MasterLife, Student Edition* goals by...

• sharing how they have seen other group members grow during *MasterLife, Student Edition;*
• reporting the kind acts they did for their new non-Christian friends;
• completing assignments for week 6;
• explaining what "take up your cross" means to them personally;
• completing memorization work on the Disciple's Cross;
• preparing for the Growing Disciples Workshop.

Standard Plan

BEFORE THE SESSION

❑ Review week 6 of *MasterLife, Student Edition.*
❑ Pray daily for each member of your group.
❑ Master this week's material in the Leader Guide.
❑ Review the goals for this session.
❑ Check with the host or hostess to be sure he or she is ready for the group this week.
❑ Arrange the meeting place so that students can sit in a circle.
❑ Have pens or pencils and extra blank paper on hand for the session.
❑ Review any last-minute plans you have made for the Growing Disciples Workshop and share them with group members.

DURING THE SESSION

Part 1 (45 minutes)

Introduction (10 minutes)

1. Greet students. Ask them to share one change they have seen in the person seated to their right since beginning *MasterLife, Student Edition.*

2. Ask each person to thank God for his or her progress in *MasterLife, Student Edition* and for the progress that the person to his or her left has mentioned.

Verifying Assignments (10 minutes)

3. Ask each student to pair up with another member to check assignments for weeks 1-6. Encourage everyone to have assignments completely checked off by the end of this session. If a student needs a few minutes to complete an assignment, arrange to meet with that person during break or after the session. Ask

students to get together to check any other incomplete assignments before the Growing Disciples Workshop.

"Minister to Others" (25 minutes)
Choose from the following list the appropriate questions and activities for your group's study. Do not exceed the time allowance.

4. Ask students to describe situations in which they have had opportunities to serve someone sacrificially (student book, p. 93). Ask members if they can remember opportunities they encountered but did not pursue. Allow two or three people to share with the group.

5. Say, **Describe what cross bearing means to you.** Ask, **What does Jesus' command to "take up your cross" mean to you personally?**

6. Ask for volunteers to describe specific, personal ways they might use the following resources in the ministries listed with each one.
   • The resource of the Word in the ministry of teaching.
   • The resource of prayer in the ministry of worship and intercession.
   • The resource of fellowship in the ministry of nurture.
   • The resource of witness in the ministry of evangelism.
   • The resources of fellowship and witness in the ministry of service.

7. Invite a volunteer to share about a time when he or she prayed regularly for a pastor or church-staff member.

8. Ask, **How do you feel when you realize Christ has said you will experience rejection when you witness in His name? How do you feel when you realize Christ has promised to send the Holy Spirit to help you?**

9. Share about a time when the Holy Spirit made you bold and gave you strength to minister to others. Then ask students to tell about their experiences in this area.

10. Ask students to discuss how they would stay connected to the Vine if their Bibles and the opportunity to pray to and worship God freely were taken away.

11. As time permits ask students to select and read a portion of *John 15* and tell in their own words what it means to them.

12. Close this part of the session by inviting members to pray. Say, **Voice a sentence prayer for yourself. Ask God to help you find ways to use the resources you have available through Him.**

Take a stand-up break. Invite students to help themselves to refreshments.

Part 2 (45 minutes)

Contacts with Non-Christian Friends (10 minutes)
1. Ask students to report on any kind acts they did last week for their new non-Christian friends. Encourage each person to participate.

2. Pray for the lost friends who have been mentioned. Pray that the group members' kind acts will be entry points for sharing the gospel when the time is appropriate.

The Disciple's Cross (15 minutes)
3. Instruct students to get in pairs to check each other's presentation of the Disciple's Cross. Remind students who are not checked off to arrange to meet with another group member during the week to present the Disciple's Cross. Each person needs to be signed off on this presentation before the Growing Disciples Workshop. In checking off the presentation, each student will be asked to quote all the verses that accompany the Disciple's Cross.

Next Week's Assignments (15 minutes)
4. Ask, **Do you have any questions about the Growing Disciples Workshop?** Distribute maps and other information as needed.

5. Urge students who may not yet have completed all their assignments to work to finish them before the Growing Disciples Workshop. At the workshop, students will be asked to share what they have learned.

6. Remind students about the Discipleship Inventory on pages 207-212 in the student book. Ask everyone to complete it before the workshop. They will score and interpret their responses at the workshop. Encourage them to be honest when completing the inventory.

7. Point out that at the Growing Disciples Workshop they will be asked to share and explain the things they have drawn to illustrate the concepts of the Disciple's Cross (p. 202). The learning activity will indicate how well they understand the truths illustrated in the Disciple's Cross.

Remind them this is not an art contest; the important thing is the concepts contained in the picture.

Closure (5 minutes)
8. Refresh students' memories about the time, date, and place for the Growing Disciples Workshop. Use the overhead cel showing the Workshop information that you prepared earlier. Finalize transportation if needed.

9. Close with prayer. Ask God to help students as they prepare to complete their work on weeks 1-6, The Disciple's Cross, of *MasterLife, Student Edition.*

AFTER THE SESSION

❏ Pray for those who are struggling to complete assignments. Pray they will use their time wisely to finish incomplete areas.

❏ Ask God to guide students as they take the Discipleship Inventory. Ask God to give them courage to be honest with their responses.

❏ Take two members with you to minister or to witness.

❏ Make final arrangements for the Growing Disciples Workshop. Contact the meeting site to confirm arrangements. Secure materials you need for the workshop.

❏ Read the plans for the Growing Disciples Workshop to evaluate the amount of final preparation you will need.

❏ Review weeks 7-12, The Disciple's Personality, in *MasterLife, Student Edition,* and be prepared to give a brief overview at the Growing Disciples Workshop.

One-to-One or Mentoring Study Plan

Follow instructions for the Standard Plan as you work with your partner. Spend extra time answering questions about the Growing Disciples Workshop and the Discipleship Inventory. Share any experiences you have had in taking the inventory and insights it gave you about your life. Pray a prayer of thanksgiving for your partner's growth in *MasterLife.*

Growing Disciples Workshop

Note to those using the One-to-One or Mentoring Study Plan: The workshop lends itself to this plan. For example, spend extra time helping the student process his or her Discipleship Inventory. Ask the individual to explain his or her Disciple's Cross concept diagram and you as leader explain the one you have drawn. Ask the student to share about changes in his or her life during MasterLife, Student Edition study; pray a prayer of thanksgiving for the changes mentioned.

> **Workshop Goals**
> By the end of this workshop, students will be able to demonstrate their progress toward MasterLife, Student Edition goals by...
> • sharing how they have seen themselves grow during MasterLife, Student Edition;
> • completing all assignments in weeks 1-6 of MasterLife, Student Edition;
> • explaining their diagram that illustrates the concepts of the Disciple's Cross;
> • completing the Discipleship Inventory and evaluating the results;
> • examining ways they plan to seek continued growth in Christ.

BEFORE THE WORKSHOP
❑ Review the basic content of weeks 7-12, The Disciple's Personality, MasterLife, Student Edition so you can give an overview at the Growing Disciples Workshop.
❑ Pray daily for each member of your group.
❑ Call each member of the group to be sure everyone will be there.
❑ Master the material in this Leader Guide for the Growing Disciples Workshop.
❑ Review the goals for the workshop.
❑ Check with the persons responsible for the meeting site to be sure they are ready for the group.
❑ Arrange the chairs so that students can sit in a circle.
❑ If you have a copy of the video that goes with the adult MasterLife study, you may choose either to show the video presentation of the Disciple's Personality or to make the presentation yourself. If you choose to present the material yourself, preview the way Avery Willis does it on the

videotape. Then develop your own script. If you choose to show the video, secure video equipment and cue the tape before the session begins.
❑ Make enough copies of "Scoring Your Inventory" (pp. 57-60) for each student to have one.
❑ Have pens, pencils, and paper on hand for the workshop.
❑ Make plans for starting the study of The Disciple's Personality, MasterLife, Student Edition. Arrange a time, date, and place for the first meeting. Be prepared to share these plans with students.
❑ Pray for the workshop. Students need to have a sense of accomplishment and success at the end of weeks 1-6 of MasterLife, Student Edition. They will get this from having all their work in "My Walk with the Master This Week" checked off and by assessing their growth as disciples.
❑ Prepare an overhead cel of the Disciple's Personality on page 105 to use for review during weeks 7-12.
❑ Prepare the following as a printed agenda to be distributed, or write it on a poster or chalkboard, or prepare an overhead cel using page 104.

> **Today's Workshop Agenda**
> • The Disciple's Cross
> • Discipleship Inventory
> • The Disciple's Personality

DURING THE WORKSHOP
Part I (60 minutes)

Icebreaker (5 minutes)
1. Greet students. Ask each person to share one change he or she has seen in himself or herself since beginning MasterLife. Go around the group until each member has responded.

2. Pray, asking each student to thank God for the progress in MasterLife that he or she has observed in group members' lives.

The Disciple's Cross (45 minutes)
3. Ask each student to show and describe his or her diagram that illustrates the concepts of the Disciple's Cross. Tell each

person to quote the Scriptures that accompany each part of the cross, as illustrated by their diagram.

4. Affirm each student's presentation after he or she finishes. Ask questions about the presentation to show interest, and encourage other members to comment or ask questions they might have. Take care to affirm each student regardless of the degree of artistic ability displayed in the drawings.

5. Post the illustrations in a prominent place in the room so everyone can enjoy them. Leave them on display the remainder of the workshop. Encourage students to study each diagram carefully.

6. Consider displaying the illustrations in a prominent place in your church after the workshop. Accompany the display with a note explaining that these illustrations are an outgrowth of the Growing Disciples Workshop. This type of display provides visual interest and serves as good promotion to attract prospective *MasterLife* members in your church.

Verifying Assignments (10 minutes)

7. Ask each student to pair up with another member. If any student still needs a few minutes to complete an assignment for weeks 1-6 in their book, such as memorizing a Scripture, take time to do this now. If both members of the pair have all their assignments checked off, use this time to practice reviewing the Scriptures they have memorized during this six weeks. Arrange to meet at break time with anyone who still needs to have an assignment checked off.

Break (15 minutes)

Part 2 (45 minutes)

Discipleship Inventory (45 minutes)

1. Ask students to turn to the Discipleship Inventory on page 207 in their student books. Ask them how they felt as they took the inventory. Say, **The Discipleship Inventory is based on the characteristics of a disciple and attempts to help you determine where you are in your growth as a disciple.**

2. Distribute copies of "Scoring Your Inventory." Allow sufficient time for students to score their inventories. Be available to answer questions.

3. Debrief what students discovered about themselves from the inventory. Discuss each of the five categories one by one using the ideas below as starters. Avoid embarrassing them by asking their scores; some will volunteer this information.
• **Attitude** Ask, **Does the list under "Attitude" on page 60 contain any characteristics that you do not think a disciple should have? Are there characteristics you would add? Which characteristic is most difficult to exemplify?**
• **Behavior** Say, **People often find that their attitudes are better than their behavior. Look at your scores for each of these two categories.** Ask, **Do you see a wide range of difference? Which is higher? What does that say to you about their relationship in your life?**
• **Relationships** Ask, **How do you relate to God based on the inventory? How do you relate to others? How important is the fellowship of other Christians?** Ask a volunteer to comment on one characteristic he or she would like to improve.
• **Ministry** Ask, **How important is it for a disciple to minister to others? What Scriptures encourage or expect ministry from Christ's disciples? Did you find your score in attitude and behavior better than in ministry? If so, what does this suggest?**
• **Doctrine** Ask, **Are there doctrines listed that you do not agree are taught in the Bible?** (Be careful not to let this become a theological debate.) Ask, **How can we live lives that demonstrate our beliefs?**

4. Read *Philippians 3:12-14* and encourage students to fulfill Paul's goal.

Break (10 minutes)

Part 3 (50 minutes)

The Disciple's Personality (45 minutes)

1. Give the Disciple's Personality presentation in your own

words or show the optional adult *MasterLife* videotape.

2. Preview weeks 7-12 of *MasterLife, Student Edition* by reviewing the weekly titles and giving a five-minute overview of the content. Lead members to decide whether to begin the sessions next week or take a week off before beginning.

3. Ask for volunteers to give personal testimonies about why they are committed to continuing the *MasterLife* study.

4. Lead a prayer for group members, asking them to commit to the Father their decision to continue with this study. Ask God to speak clearly to them about His will for them.

Closure (5 minutes)

5. Congratulate members on completing weeks 1-6 in *MasterLife, Student Edition*. Assure them that the time investment they have made in learning to be a follower of Christ will make their pilgrimage more meaningful in the days ahead. Express appreciation for each member.

6. Close with prayer. Invite each student to pray, thanking God for walking side by side with him or her through weeks 1-6 of *MasterLife, Student Edition*.

AFTER THE WORKSHOP

❑ Write a note to each student expressing appreciation for his or her participation in the course. Remind each student that you are praying as he or she continues to apply concepts of *MasterLife, Student Edition* to daily life.

❑ Finalize your plans for continuing with weeks 7-12 of *MasterLife, Student Edition*, "The Disciple's Personality." Confirm the meeting site.

❑ This is a good time to take stock of the leadership you provided during weeks 1-6 of *MasterLife, Student Edition*. If you believe that a problem exists between you and one of the members, visit with this person and seek reconciliation.

❑ Spend time in prayer for each student.

❑ Through bulletins and announcements inform the church of the *MasterLife* group's progress and expectations. Ask students to share brief testimonies about what *MasterLife* has meant to them.

Scoring Your Inventory [1]

The Discipleship Inventory detects strengths and weaknesses in your discipleship development. You will access your discipleship development by transferring your responses to five categories: attitudes, behavior, relationships, ministry, and doctrine.

Taking the inventory once is valuable because it gives you a beginning point for growth. Knowing where you are in each category allows you to determine the areas you need to work on. The inventory becomes even more valuable when you complete it again after a period of time. Comparing your scores in each of the five categories will indicate your degree of growth. The combined score will provide an indicator of total growth. Use the following directions to score your inventory.

1. Transfer your responses from the inventory to the scoring chart on the following two pages. Some questions are reverse-response questions. These questions are noted with an asterisk on the scoring chart. When tabulating the scores for questions 13, 20, 31, 36, 40, 56, 58, 60, 61, 65, and 84, the score should be reversed: 5=1, 4=2, 3=3, 2=4, 1=5. Numbers 136-141 and 143-152 are not required for scoring.
2. Add the values of your responses for each category and write the number in the blank labeled "Total." Divide by the number indicated and write the number in the box.
3. To calculate your combined total, add the "Totals" for each category (not the numbers in the boxes) and divide by 150. Write your combined total in the box provided.
4. On the chart below, shade each bar graph to represent your total for each category. Shade the combined-total bar to picture your overall score. Categories in which you made low scores are areas for growth in discipleship.
5. Review the descriptions on page 60 for each of the five categories. These brief summaries identify areas you might consider working on to further your growth in discipleship.

CATEGORY AVERAGE

		Attitudes	Behavior	Relationships	Ministry	Doctrine	Combined total
5 / 4	Maturing						
3	Growing						
2	Developing						
1	Young						
0	New						

[1]Steve McCord, James Slack, and Emily Yeatts, "The Discipleship Inventory" (Richmond: The International Mission Board of the Southern Baptist Convention). Used and adapted by permission.

Discipleship Inventory

Attitudes	Behavior	Relationships	Ministry	Doctrine
1_____	1_____			
3_____	2_____			
		5_____	4_____	
6_____		6_____		
			7_____	
			8_____	
			9_____	
10_____				
		11_____	12_____	
		12_____		
		13_____*		
		14_____		
		15_____		
17_____		17_____	16_____	
			18_____	
		19_____		
		20_____*		
			21_____	
		22_____		
		23_____		
		24_____		
		25_____		
		26_____	26_____	
			27_____	
29_____				28_____
		30_____		
				31_____*
33_____			32_____	
			34_____	
				35_____
36_____*				
				37_____
				38_____
			39_____	
				40_____*
	41_____		41_____	
	42_____			
			43_____	
			44_____	
	45_____			
	46_____			
	47_____			
	48_____			
49_____				
		50_____		
		51_____		
		52_____		
		53_____		
	54_____	54_____		
	55_____			
		56_____*		
		57_____		
	58_____*		58_____*	
	59_____			
		60_____*		
		61_____*		
	62_____			
		63_____		
		64_____		
			65_____*	
	66_____			
	67_____			
	68_____			
	69_____			
		70_____		

Attitudes	Behavior	Relationships	Ministry	Doctrine
		71_____	72_____	
			73_____	
		74_____	75_____	
			76_____	
			77_____	
			78_____	
			79_____	
80_____	80_____			
81_____				82_____
82_____				
83_____		84_____*	85_____	
				86_____
87_____	88_____			
		89_____		
				90_____
				91_____
			92_____	
			93_____	
			94_____	
			95_____	
			96_____	
			97_____	
	99_____	98_____		
		100_____		
			101_____	
		102_____		
	104_____	103_____		
			105_____	
		106_____		
			107_____	
			108_____	
		109_____		
	110_____			
111_____		112_____		
113_____		113_____		
115_____			114_____	
116_____				
117_____				
118_____			118_____	
119_____				
120_____			120_____	
		121_____		
		122_____		
		123_____		
		124_____		
		125_____		
		126_____		126_____
				127_____
				128_____
				129_____
				130_____
				131_____
				132_____
				133_____
				134_____
				135_____
				142_____

Total _____ +	_____ +	_____ +	_____ +	_____ =	_____
Divide by 22=	Divide by 22=	Divide by 46=	Divide by 39=	Divide by 21=	Divide by 150=
☐	☐	☐	☐	☐	☐

Categories in the Discipleship Inventory

ATTITUDES

A disciple ...

- possesses a desire and willingness to learn.
- lives according to biblical principles and guidelines.
- repents after violating Scripture.
- forfeits personal desires and conveniences, if necessary, to meet the needs of others.
- practices humility (transparent and honest about weaknesses).
- lives a life of integrity (personal life matches public image).
- is accountable to others.

BEHAVIOR

A disciple ...

- utilizes time and talent for God's purposes.
- adapts attitudes and actions to conform to biblical standards.
- acts appropriately toward the opposite sex.

RELATIONSHIPS

A disciple ...

- accepts and values himself or herself as created in the image of God.
- experiences an awareness of God's presence through the ministry of the Holy Spirit.
- trusts God in difficult times, as well as in good times.
- seeks to commune with and learn about God by hearing, reading, studying, memorizing God's Word, and through regular prayer.
- consistently fellowships with other believers in the context of a local church.
- builds meaningful relationships with other believers beyond his or her local church.
- maintains a forgiving spirit when wronged.
- confesses or asks forgiveness when guilty of an offense.

MINISTRY

A disciple ...

- publicly identifies with Christ and with the church when given the opportunity.
- seeks and takes advantage of opportunities to share the gospel with others.
- ministers to other believers.
- seeks the good of all people through a willingness to meet practical needs.

DOCTRINE

A disciple ...

- believes that each person inherited a sinful nature as a result of Adam's fall and is separated from God and in need of a Savior.
- believes that God fully revealed Himself through His Son, Jesus Christ, who died for the sins of the world, was raised from the dead, and will personally come a second time.
- trusts only and totally in Christ for salvation.
- experiences the Holy Spirit's complete entrance at the time of the new birth.
- looks to Jesus Christ for eternal security.
- accepts and follows the Bible as the authoritative and completely reliable revelation of God.
- believes that the church is God's means for nurturing believers, preserving doctrine, and carrying out His plan for spreading the gospel.
- believes that heaven is the final home of believers and that hell is the final place of all who have never accepted Jesus Christ as Savior.

MASTERLIFE
STUDENT EDITION
LEADER GUIDE

"I have come that they may have life, and have it to the full" (John 10:10).

In *MasterLife, Student Edition*, weeks 7-12, God will use The Disciple's Personality
to lead students to develop Christlikeness in character
as they learn to live in the Spirit.

Contents—Weeks 7-12 and Testimony Workshop

GROUP SESSION 7

Do God's Will

Session Goals

By the end of this session, students will be able to demonstrate their commitment to *MasterLife, Student Edition* by...

- stating goals for their study of *MasterLife, Student Edition*;
- explaining the Natural Person part of the Disciple's Personality;
- praying for lost friends that group members have named;
- saying from memory *Philippians 2:13*;
- describing three requirements for doing God's will;
- completing the assignments for week 7.

Standard Plan

BEFORE THE SESSION

❏ Review week 7 and read and complete the learning activities for week 7 of *MasterLife, Student Edition* to stay ahead of the group.

❏ Study week 8 and do the exercises in the student book. You will preview week 8 for the group at the end of this session.

❏ Find a quiet time and place to pray for group members by name. Ask the Lord to give you wisdom to prepare and lead the group session.

❏ Read "During the Session."

❏ Have at least five lost persons on your Prayer-Covenant List and be prepared to discuss this activity with students.

❏ Arrange for refreshments to be served during the session.

❏ Arrange in a circle chairs for everyone in the group.

❏ Have pens or pencils and extra blank paper on hand for the session.

❏ Plan to stay within the times given for each part. Print an agenda with the subjects and times listed. This helps the group stay on schedule.

Allowing students to share freely is far more important than sticking legalistically to a plan you develop for the group session. Students sometimes arrive at a session eager to tell about something that happened in their lives during the week related to that week's content. Be sensitive to this need, and be flexible. Allow God to work in your group, providing opportunities for everyone to respond during the session.

DURING THE SESSION

Part 1 (45 minutes)

Introduction (10 minutes)

1. Welcome each student and point them to the refreshments. As leader, express

genuine interest in students as they arrive. Tell them how glad you are they are participating in the *MasterLife* study. Visit informally until time to begin.

2. Begin and end promptly. Remind the group that you will begin and end each session on time. Allow students to fellowship or talk after the sessions.

3. Ask each student to give a one-sentence statement of his or her goals for this course. Call the group to prayer. Ask students to say a sentence prayer asking God to help them achieve their goals.

"Do God's Will" (30 minutes)
Choose from the following list appropriate questions and activities for your group. Watch your time.

4. Ask, **How does God's will differ from a person's will?** (See the answer on p. 107-8.) **Why does God want you to do His will? What is His primary purpose for your life?** *(To bring glory to God. Many other reasons may be given, but they all bring glory to God.)*

5. Ask, **How did Jesus fulfill His vision of God's purpose for His life?** *(He died to redeem humanity.)* Ask volunteers to state their vision of God's purpose for their lives.

6. Ask one student to share his or her answer to the first activity in day 3. Discuss the difficulties in doing God's will. Then ask, **How does God provide the resources for doing His will?**

"In the Carpenter's Shop" (5 minutes)
7. Ask a volunteer to sum up some of the tendencies of the old life. Ask another volunteer to sum up some of the tendencies of the new life. Close in prayer, asking God to help members develop Christlike character during this study.

Take a break. Invite students to help themselves to refreshments.

Part 2 (45 minutes)

Prayer Time (5 minutes)
1. Ask each student to pair with another person. Say, **Briefly summarize your experiences this week. Share with your partner the names of five lost persons on your prayer list. Pray for the people on your partner's list.**

Presentation: The Natural Person (15 minutes)
2. Remind group members that they are expanding the circle in the center of the Disciple's Cross to show how they can make Christ the Lord of their total personalities. Give a brief overview of the Disciple's Personality presented at the Growing Disciples Workshop.

3. Instruct each person to present to another person in his or her own words the Natural Person part of the Disciple's Personality. If they give the majority of the ideas correctly, the partner should draw an upright line in the diamond on "Minister to Others" in "My Walk with the Master This Week." Students are not expected to have learned the rest of the presentation. The Disciple's Personality is to be mastered a section at a time over a four-week period. Encourage them to use any extra time to check on other assignments.

Discussion: The Natural Person (5 minutes)

4. Ask volunteers to share answers to the following questions:
  • What causes you to inherit a nature that is inclined toward sin?
  • Why can't good deeds alone cause a person in the flesh to please God?
  • What happens when the big I in your personality takes over in your life?
  • What part of your personality gives additional evidence that you were created in the image of God?

Principles of Conversational Prayer (15 minutes)

5. Introduce conversational prayer. Say, **The most common mistakes are using us and we; moving to a new subject before everyone has had a chance to pray about the current subject; using formal terms of address for God; and not praying short prayers.** Ask students to pray conversationally in groups of four. After they finish, tell them that they will review "Principles of Conversational Prayer" in next week's lesson.

Next Week's Assignments (5 minutes)

6. Ask students to look at "My Walk with the Master This Week" for week 8 and review the specific assignments. Remind them again that as they complete an assignment, they will draw a vertical line through the diamond. A fellow member will verify their work during session 8 and draw a horizontal line through the diamond to form a cross.

7. Preview the content of week 8 briefly. Ask students to complete the activities in "Renew Your Mind" before next week's session. Say,
  • **You will be asked to begin having a daily quiet time 21 consecutive days. The purpose of the 21-day goal is to establish a daily quiet time as a regular pattern in your schedule.**
  • **You will receive an assignment to go out to dinner or plan a private time with a close friend. This assignment is designed to contribute to the health of relationships within the body of Christ.**
  • **You will also be asked to do something good for a non-Christian member of your immediate or extended family. Don't overlook unsaved family members when you are thinking about those who need the good news of Christ.**

8. Elaborate on "In the Carpenter's Shop" from last week. Say, **These activities, which occur several times during each week's work, are designed to help you determine ways that you need to become more like Christ.**

Closure (5 minutes)

9. Close with prayer. Invite students to stand and join hands in a prayer of dismissal. Ask them to voice a one-sentence prayer for the person on their left, especially as that person relates to non-Christian family members during the coming week. Express gratitude that you are part of the group, and request students' prayers for you as you serve them during the weeks that follow.

AFTER THE SESSION

❑ Before the next group session pray for each member specifically.

❑ Call each student and encourage him or her in their study. Answer any questions they may have, and encourage anyone who seems to need it. Thank them for their commitment.

❑ Use the following questions to evaluate your leadership.
  • Was I thoroughly prepared?
  • Was my presentation clear?
  • Did I follow the Leader Guide?
  • Did I provide positive leadership?
  • Was I a servant leader?
  • Did I create a group environment?
  • Did I help students communicate with each other?
  • Do students understand the purpose of the study?
  • Was I enthusiastic about how God will use *MasterLife* in students' lives and our church?

❑ Read "Before the Session" for Group Session 8 to evaluate the amount of preparation you will need. At the top of the first page of Group Session 8 material, record when you will prepare.

❑ Carefully study week 9 and do all the exercises in the student book. You will preview week 9 for members during session 8.

One-to-One or Mentoring Study Plan

Part 1

1. Follow directions for the Standard Plan. Use your time to learn about this student and how you can best help him or her. Avoid lecturing to the person; allow him or her to discover answers as you work together.

2. Ask the student to quote *Philippians 2:13,* the verse he or she memorized during the week. Review "Do God's Will." Explore the student's vision of God's purpose for his or her life. Share your vision of God's purpose for your life. Share any insight you may have for the person's life. Share a Bible promise you would claim for the person. Discuss parts of your personalities that might not be fully committed to God. Read verses that help you commit each part of your personality to God.

3. Discuss the problem of doing God's will even though you are committed to

Christ. Talk about the two natures people have. Discuss God's provision for helping you do His will.

4. Discuss the segment "In the Carpenter's Shop." Because you are working one-to-one, you can spend more time helping the person understand the principles of developing Christlike character. Tell about experiences in setting aside old ways and putting on new traits.

Part 2
Ask the student to present the material on the Natural Person part of the Disciple's Personality. Follow the Standard Plan for reviewing week 8 assignments.

GROUP SESSION 8

Renew Your Mind

Session Goals

By the end of this session, students will be able to demonstrate their progress in achieving the *MasterLife, Student Edition* goals by…
- having a date or private time with a close friend;
- completing assignments for week 8;
- explaining the Worldly Christian part of the Disciple's Personality;
- identifying ways to renew their minds and committing themselves to a course of action;
- praying, using "Principles of Conversational Prayer";
- praying for group members' family members who do not know Christ.

Standard Plan

BEFORE THE SESSION

❑ Review week 8 and read and complete the activities for week 9 in *MasterLife, Student Edition.*

❑ Pray daily for each member of the group. Ask the Lord to give you wisdom to prepare for and lead the group session.

❑ Read carefully "During the Session."

❑ Review the goals for this session.

❑ Check with the host or hostess about refreshments for the group this week.

❑ Arrange the meeting place so that students can sit in a circle.

❑ Have pens or pencils and extra blank paper on hand for the session.

❑ Be prepared to report on your "date" time spent with a friend.

❑ Master "How to Listen to God's Word" on pages 147 in the student book so you can teach it to the group. Be prepared to refer to the Hearing the Word form (pp. 220-21) during the session.

❑ Get a 10 or 12 penny nail or a sharp pencil for each person.

❑ As you prepare to train students using "Testimony Outline" (p. 153), review your personal testimony to be sure it meets the guidelines. Be prepared to share your testimony without notes and to tell students how you prepared your testimony according to the outline provided in the student book.

❑ Begin to make plans for the Testimony Workshop that follows session 12. Ask the group the best time and place for the workshop. The workshop will last three hours. You might want to meet at some time other than in the evening. Meet at the church or at a place where students can work individually at tables while you help others in the group with their testimonies. Perhaps a Saturday morning or afternoon or a Sunday afternoon would be appropriate.

❑ Enlist someone to help you listen to testimonies as students prepare them. This can be a respected member of your church, someone who has completed *MasterLife,* or a current group member who is demonstrating maturity in discipleship.

❏ OPTIONAL: You can train this helper by showing him or her the adult *MasterLife* video segment on evaluating testimonies. Week 9 instructions will guide you in how this person can help you.

❏ Preview the videotape on testimonies. Practice evaluating the testimonies on the videotape.

❏ Review the following general instructions in your preparation.
  • Don't be critical of students who have not memorized the Scripture-memory verses word-perfect, but each week encourage them to work toward the mastery of each verse.
  • Don't reprimand those who have problems completing assignments. Praise them for what they do; ask others to share insights that might be helpful in completing assignments. Encourage students to bear each other's burdens.

DURING THE SESSION
Part 1 (45 minutes)

Getting Started (5 minutes)
1. Greet students as they arrive. Begin on time. Be alert to signs of progress or any problems students may be facing. Open the session with prayer. Ask for special prayer requests.

My Walk with the Master This Week (15 minutes)
2. Ask students to pair with someone to check "My Walk with the Master This Week." They will ask the other person if he or she did the assignment. In some cases the student verifying may ask to see the work done. Members must quote memory verses correctly before this item is marked as verified.

Private Time (10 minutes)
3. Divide your group in half (groups of four to six persons). Invite students in each small group to share experiences they had when they went out to dinner or spent private time with a close friend. Ask volunteers to tell what areas of growth they saw in the relationship during this time.

Conversational Prayer (10 minutes)
4. Say, **Stay in your small groups and discuss the key elements of conversational prayer.**

5. Ask students to share experiences they had during the week in praying conversationally with family, a friend, or a prayer partner.

6. Invite students to pray conversationally. Ask them to start praying without anyone making requests. As they mention requests in their prayers, others can pray for the same thing.

"Renew Your Mind" (20 minutes)
7. Remind students of the importance of completing all exercises and learning the

materials before they attend the group session. The purpose for discussing the study in the group session is to reflect on it, explore the subject further, and apply it.

8. Say, **In an age of mass media, Madison-Avenue advertising, and mood-control drugs, the question of who controls your mind is relevant. Does a non-Christian have a choice about who or what controls his or her mind?** After several responses, call on a volunteer to read *Romans 7:18-20,24.* Ask, **So who is in control?** *(Sin is in control.)*

9. Ask, **Does a Christian have a choice about who or what controls his or her mind?** *(Yes, the person can choose to let God control instead of letting sin control.)* Ask students to suggest verses that support their answers. Verses might include *2 Corinthians 10:5* and *Colossians 2:2.* Say, **Not all Christians allow God to control their minds. God may have input but not have control.**

10. Use the following analogy: **Sheep in Bible days were trained to respond to the voice of their shepherd. Shepherds could graze their flocks together during the day. But at night each shepherd called his flock aside. The sheep responded because they knew their master's voice. We are to be trained to respond only to the voice of God.** Ask a volunteer to read *John 10:2-5.*

11. Ask, **Does letting Christ have control of our minds mean we are giving up part of our mental or intellectual capacities?** *(Since Christ is the author and sustainer of truth and reality, to be controlled by Him should increase our understanding of truth and reality.)*

12. Ask a student to read *2 Corinthians 10:5.* Ask, **What are some worldly imaginations or arguments that can obstruct the knowledge of God?** Write students' responses on a chalkboard or something large enough for everyone to see. Responses should include secular ideas, entertainment, television, magazines, books, and pictures. Ask, **How can we keep these things from obstructing our knowledge of God?** After several have responded, ask, **What are some positive ways you can make your thoughts obedient to Christ?** Add students' responses to the list. Responses should include prayer, Bible study, following the Spirit's leadership, worship, and Christian fellowship.

13. Say, **A college student was having a difficult time keeping a pure mind. A friend accompanied him to his room to counsel with him about the problem. Every wall of the student's room had nude pictures from pornographic magazines. Ask, What was the first piece of advice the friend should have given the student?**

14. Read *Philippians 4:8* from several translations. List words or phrases that mean the same as the words in this verse, such as *pure* and *lovely.* Ask, **What are we to do about things that are *pure* and *lovely*?** *(Think on them.)*

15. Sum up the key to mind control by asking, **Why is the Bible important in renewing your mind?** *(It is God's revealed truth that has the power to change lives through mind renewal.)*

16. Discuss how meditation on memorized Scriptures renews our minds. Suggest that students listen to passages of recorded Scriptures. They may make their own recordings or purchase them.

17. Ask volunteers to share the commitments they made to get God's Word into their lives daily.

18. Emphasize that this study should not leave students with the impression that being God-centered, as opposed to being controlled by evil, makes us pawns. Each person determines to whom he or she will give control, and control is exercised only as the individual allows it to happen. Say, **Yes, each person has a choice about the control that will be exercised over him or her. And that person is responsible and accountable to God for the choices he or she makes.**

Take a break and invite students to have some of the refreshments.

Part 2 (45 minutes)

Prayer Time (10 minutes)
1. Ask students to share specific prayer requests related to their week 8 assignment to do something kind for a student of their immediate or extended family who does not know Christ.

2. Briefly discuss "In the Carpenter's Shop." Ask a volunteer to share an area in which the Holy Spirit is helping him or her become more Christlike and to put off old habits. Pray, thanking God for what was just shared as representative of what is occurring in the lives of members.

The Worldly Christian (10 minutes)
3. Invite students to find a partner. Instruct each person to present to the other in his or her own words the Worldly Christian part of the Disciple's Personality. If they give most of the idea correctly, their partner should draw the horizontal line on the diamond in the "Minister to Others" segment of "My Walk with the Master This Week." Students are not expected to have learned the rest of the presentation. Remember that the Disciple's Personality is to be mastered a section at a time over a four-week period. Members can use any extra time to check on other assignments.

"How to Listen to God's Word" (10 minutes)
4. Use *James 1:22-25* as the key passage as you explain "How to Listen to God's Word" on pages 147 in the student book.

5. Ask students to use the questions based on the parable of the sower *(Matt. 13:3-23)* to determine what kind of hearers they usually are. Invite them to tell the group which classification they fall in.

6. Review the instructions based on *James 1.*

7. Ask members to look at the Hearing the Word form in the student book on page 220. Describe how to take notes on a sermon. Use the notes that you took this week as a model.

8. Encourage students to take notes on sermons and Sunday School lessons. Suggest that they begin a file of notes for future reference.

Testimony Outline (10 minutes)
9. Ask students to define and illustrate the word *testimony*. (Many television commercials use the testimony approach to sell products.)

10. Distinguish between the basic salvation testimony and other testimonies of the Christian life. Say, **The testimony we will be working with during weeks 7-12 will be the salvation testimony. This testimony forms the foundation of all other Christian testimonies. Its length and use depend on the situation.**

11. Ask students to turn to "Testimony Outline" on page 153 in the student book. Go over this material carefully and call attention to the assignment to write four facts about their conversions. Say, **In week 10 you will build on this basic outline to develop your testimony further.**

12. Give your personal testimony as a model for the members of the group. Be sure it is not longer than three or four minutes. After you have given your testimony, ask students to identify in it the points of the basic testimony outline.

13. Tell the group about the Testimony Workshop that will take place at the end of session 12. This will be a three-hour workshop. If you know the date for the workshop, announce it so students can put it on their calendars. If you have not set a date and the date is open for discussion, discuss with them various times, dates, and places. Encourage students to work on their testimonies between now and then. For many of them, this will be one of the most difficult assignments they do during this training. It will also be one of the most important.

14. Remind students that as part of this week's work, they are to share with a Christian friend the steps they've taken in beginning to outline their personal testimony.

Next Week's Assignments (5 minutes)
15. Ask students to look at "My Walk with the Master This Week" for week 9 on page 138 in the student book. Review the specific assignments. Distribute the

large nails or sharp pencils. Call attention to the instructions in the student book for using them.

16. Address any problems or questions students may have. Praise them for their progress and encourage them to keep up the good work.

17. Announce the meeting time and place for next week. Close with prayer. Ask God to help each student place Christ first in their lives during the week ahead.

AFTER THE SESSION
☐ Evaluate the session by listing what you believe was effective. Consider ways to improve future sessions.
☐ Evaluate the response of individual students to the teaching on renewing their minds. Talk with anyone you think needs personal help at this time.
☐ Look for opportunities to praise students sincerely, particularly any who may be experiencing problems. Offer your help as needed.
☐ Invite two members to visit or to minister with you during the week. Don't ask them to do anything they are not experienced in doing. The purpose is for them to observe. Before each visit, tell them what you expect to find and do. After the visit, talk about why you conducted the visit as you did. Use the Roman Road gospel presentation (pp. 83-87) when you witness each week so the students can become familiar with it before they are asked to learn it.
☐ Read "Before the Session" for Group Session 9. Evaluate the amount of preparation you will need for the next group session. At the top of the first page of session 9, record when you will prepare.
☐ Carefully study week 10 and do all the exercises in the student book. You will preview week 10 for students during session 9.

One-to-One or Mentoring Study Plan

Follow instructions in the Standard Plan. Make the following adjustments for the one-to-one relationship.

Part 1
1. Lead the study "Renew Your Mind." Be frank about the battle you have in keeping your mind on the right kind of thoughts. Ask where your one-to-one partner has problems. Share things you have found helpful in renewing your mind.

2. Share experiences you have had with conversational prayer. Ask the student to share experiences he or she had in praying conversationally with a family member, friend, or prayer partner this week. Pray conversationally with the person you are discipling.

Part 2
1. Present the material related to the Worldly Christian part of the Disciple's Personality and ask the student to note anything that is different from the presenta-

tion in the student book. Ask the person to present the material on the Worldly Christian.

2. Preview next week's assignments. Explain "How to Listen to God's Word." Share with your partner experiences you have had in listening to sermons since you began using the Hearing the Word form and applying the principles.

Master Your Emotions

Session Goals

By the end of this session, students will be able to demonstrate their progress toward *MasterLife, Student Edition* goals by...
- listing the four parts of a salvation testimony;
- completing week 9 assignments;
- explaining the Spiritual Christian part of the Disciple's Personality;
- praying for group members' requests regarding their testimonies or their sharing with a friend;
- describing how they benefitted from taking notes on a sermon;
- naming the six steps of the ACTION plan for mastering their emotions;
- applying the principles of mastering emotions to a case study;
- relating and applying previous weeks' studies to the Disciple's Personality.

Standard Plan

BEFORE THE SESSION

❑ Review week 9 and read and complete the learning activities for week 10 of *MasterLife, Student Edition.*

❑ Call students who are having problems completing assignments to ask them how they are doing this week and to encourage them.

❑ Master this week's material in the Leader Guide.

❑ Review the goals for this session.

❑ Check with the host or hostess to be sure he or she is ready for the group this week.

❑ Arrange the meeting place so that students can sit in a circle.

❑ Have pens or pencils and extra blank paper on hand for the session.

❑ Review in the student book, "Guidelines for Writing Your Testimony" (p. 160). In part 2 of this session you will help students prepare to gather materials for their testimonies during week 10 in order to write their testimonies before Group Session 11. Be prepared to encourage and affirm the work each member has done so far so they can take the next step toward writing their full testimonies.

❑ Contact the person you have enlisted to help you in the testimony preparation time. Ask the person to be present during this week's session. Instructions for what this person is to do appear on page 77 and 98.

❑ If students have not kept up with their assignments using the Standard Plan or will not be able to give the Disciple's Personality successfully by week 10's group session, you may want to extend week 10 assignments over the next two weeks. Decide now so you can give the proper instructions for the plan you will use this week.

❑ Review the weekly studies to date and relate them to the Disciple's Personality.

❑ Have coffee or a soft drink with someone you do not like or with someone who does not like you. Be prepared to report on your experiences to the group.

DURING THE SESSION
Part 1 (45 minutes)

Introduction (25 minutes)
1. Begin the session on time even if all members are not present. During the presentation time ask students to share their progress on overcoming problems in their work on their testimonies.

2. Begin with prayer. Ask students for reports on their experience in spending some time with someone they do not like or with a person who does not like them. Share your experience first; then invite others to share. Ask students to pray a sentence prayer for the person on his or her right pertaining to a request that person mentioned about sharing with a friend.

"My Walk with the Master This Week" (10 minutes)
3. Invite students to get with another person to quote *Galatians 5:22-23* to each other. While students work in pairs, they can check each other's "My Walk with the Master This Week" and make the horizontal mark in the boxes after verifying work. Encourage them to share with their partners their strong and weak points in completing assignments.

Prayer Time (5 minutes)
4. Ask students to mention specific praises they have regarding their experiences in listening to a sermon this past week. Invite them to share with the group how they used the Hearing the Word form. Suggest that volunteers pray short prayers of thanksgiving for the items mentioned. Pray a brief prayer and invite others to pray also.

"Master Your Emotions" (20 minutes)
Choose from the following list appropriate questions and activities for your group to review the study. Watch your time.

5. Use the first 5 to 10 minutes to relate previous weeks' studies to the Disciple's Personality.
   • Ask students the significance of studying the will in "Do God's Will" first before you studied the other parts of the personality. (The will is central and determines what a person does.)
   • Ask students to recall ways you are to renew your mind. Ask them how they think the renewing of a person's mind pertains to the Disciple's Personality.

6. Ask students what role emotions play in letting Christ master a person's life. Ask whether emotions are bad or good. *(Emotions themselves are not harmful. How a person responds to them can be harmful.)* Then ask, **On what are emotions**

usually based? *(Values or beliefs.)*

- Ask, **Do you agree or disagree with the statements that "emotions are spontaneous responses to your values and beliefs. Over the years your emotional responses have been either affirmed or challenged"? Why?**

7. Ask students, without referring to their books, to name the six steps in the ACTION plan for mastering their emotions.

8. Ask members to role-play the following true situation that one *MasterLife* member faced the week he was studying "Master Your Emotions." Select members to role-play the following characters: the man, his wife, their 13-year-old daughter, the store owner, and a member of the gang. They will role-play the scene twice. The first time they should role-play the emotional responses as worldly Christians might respond. The second time they should role-play how spiritual Christians might respond. In both cases the emotions are quite real.

Wert Campbell, a *MasterLife* group member, opposed the opening of a liquor store in his community. He organized a petition to prevent it. The licensing committee agreed with the petition and denied the liquor store's request. Three months later, the man bought a quick-food store and applied again for the liquor license. Wert visited the police station to see what could be done. The next morning at 4:45 Wert received an anonymous phone call. The caller told Wert if he did not back off, he would be taken care of. Emotions of fear and anger surged through Wert as he lay awake in bed. His wife talked to him about the situation. Fifteen minutes later a different anonymous caller said he was a member of "the gang" and if Wert persisted in opposing them, they would burn down his house. Wert knew they were capable of doing this and that he would be tempted to shoot them if they tried. The second time the phone rang, his 13-year-old daughter came to the bedroom and asked who called.

After they finish the role plays, tell them that Wert reacted as a spiritual Christian, the license was again denied, and Wert invited the man to his home and witnessed to him.

9. Discuss the role play. Discuss how the ACTION steps for mastering your emotions could be used. Ask volunteers to share their experiences of applying the ACTION steps to mastering an emotion this week. Voice a prayer asking God to help group members master their emotions.

Take a stand-up break. Invite participants to help themselves to refreshments.

Part 2 (45 minutes)

The Spiritual Christian (15 minutes)

1. Ask students to pair with a person he or she has not yet worked with and pre-

sent the Spiritual Christian section of the Disciple's Personality to each other.

2. Say, **If your partner gives most of the ideas correctly, make a horizontal mark in the diamond box in the section in "My Walk with the Master This Week." Remember that you are not expected to have learned the rest of the presentation. The Disciple's Personality is to be mastered a section at a time over a four-week period.**

3 Ask volunteers to share answers to the following questions:
- **How does a spiritual Christian master his or her emotions?**
- **How have you been aware in the past week of the Holy Spirit's giving you the ability to control your emotions?**

"In the Carpenter's Shop" (5 minutes)
4. Ask, **Would someone volunteer to share what is being removed from your life and what is being added as the Holy Spirit helps you become more Christlike?** After someone shares, pray a prayer of thanksgiving for what the person has shared and for growth others have experienced.

Testimony Outlines (20 minutes)
5. The first half of this time period, arrange students in small groups of four. Review testimony outlines. Each person should "talk through" the basic facts of his or her testimony outlined during the work on "Testimony Outline." Ask them to be brief (three minutes) and factual. They will not be sharing full testimonies at this point but are simply discussing the basic facts they have written down.

6. For the second half of this time period, work as a total group. Call attention to "Guidelines for Writing Your Testimony" on page 153 in the student book. Highlight suggestions that apply to problems that surfaced during the testimony-outline practice. Alert students to the following common errors of testimony writing so they can avoid them as they build their background information. They will write their testimonies before Group Session 11.
- Not focusing on the salvation testimony. Other testimonies are appropriate for other people at other times, but the testimony they are writing is one to be shared with non-Christians.
- Reminiscing too much about things that would not be interesting to others.
- Sounding like a "holy Joe or Jane" who has all the answers.
- Too long.
- Either too specific about ages, places, and churches or so general that the testimony does not sound real.

7. Break students into groups of two to four people to talk through "Testimony Outline." Utilize the person you enlisted to help you by listening and making suggestions in the groups you are not in.

8. Remind students about the time and place for the Testimony Workshop at the end of session 12. Ask them if they have any questions about the workshop.

Next Week's Assignments (5 minutes)

9. Ask students to look at "My Walk with the Master This Week" for week 10 on page 155 and review the specific assignments. Make sure they understand how they are to complete each assignment.

10. Briefly preview the content of week 10. Ask students to complete the material "Present Your Body" before the next session.

11. Review the assignment about taking notes from a sermon as you continue to use the Hearing the Word form. Urge members to be on the alert for sermon references to the theme of presenting your body as a living sacrifice, the topic of week 10.

12. Call attention to the Who Are You? and Steps to Victorious Living parts of the Disciple's Personality they are to learn during next week's study. Explain that this material will help them recognize which portion of the Disciple's Personality describes them as they are today and will show steps they can take to be all Christ wants them to be.

13. Announce the time and place for the next meeting. Note the importance of 21 consecutive days of quiet times. Remind students that if they have not completed this assignment, they need to begin at the start of week 10 in order to have 21 consecutive days by the end of week 12.

14. Stand, join hands, and offer a prayer of dismissal. Ask each student to voice a one-sentence prayer for the person on his or her right. Say, **Ask God to help this member grow in his or her relationship with Him through *MasterLife*.**

AFTER THE SESSION

❏ Meet individually or in small groups with students who seemed to be having problems with the basic testimony outline.
❏ Encourage students who may be lagging behind in their assignments. Help them with any problems. If necessary, enlist another student to work with them.
❏ Take one or two members witnessing. You may want to visit some of the non-Christian persons whom they have listed on their Prayer-Covenant Lists. Model how to use your personal testimony.
❏ Pray for each student, using specific verses as the basis of your prayers. You may want to share with each person the verse you claimed for him or her. This could be done by card, telephone, or personal contact.
❏ Read "Before the Session" for Group Session 10 to evaluate the amount of time you will need to prepare for the next group session. Record at the top of the first page of the Group Session 10 material when you will prepare.
❏ Carefully study week 11 and do all the exercises in the student book. You will preview week 11 for students during session 10.

One-to-One or Mentoring Study Plan

Part 1

Along with the Standard Plan, help the person share particular emotions that he or she has difficulty mastering so that you can work with him or her in discovering Christ-honoring options. Be honest about the difficulties you have and share solutions that have worked for you.

Part 2

Give individual time to help this person share the story of his or her life with you so that you can recommend the best facts to use in a salvation testimony. Share any challenges you may have faced in learning to write your testimony.

Present Your Body

Session Goals

By the end of this session, students will be able to demonstrate their progress toward *MasterLife, Student Edition* goals by...
- sharing ways they are becoming more Christlike in character;
- completing week 10 assignments;
- giving the entire presentation of the Disciple's Personality to another group member;
- applying to their lives the teaching of the study on the use of their bodies;
- praying about their victories and personal needs as well as those of others;
- sharing experiences of discussing with a friend their testimony preparation;
- preparing background material from which to write their testimonies before session 11;
- helping other students identifying the key facts in preparing to write personal testimonies.

Standard Plan

BEFORE THE SESSION

❑ Review week 10 and read and complete the learning activities for week 11 of *MasterLife, Student Edition.*

❑ Pray daily for your group members. Some may become discouraged as the amount of work to accomplish before a session increases. Ask God for guidance and encouragement in each student's life.

❑ Master this week's material in the Leader Guide.

❑ Review the goals for this session.

❑ Check with the host or hostess to be sure he or she is ready for the group this week.

❑ Arrange the meeting place so that students can sit in a circle.

❑ Have pens or pencils, extra blank paper, and newsprint or a chalkboard on hand for activities.

❑ Review memory verses to date to be sure that you know them.

❑ Draw on newsprint or the chalkboard the basic picture of the Disciple's Personality as it appears in the student book (p. 167). Be sure to leave space to add the extra words between the circle and the words *God, Satan.* You will use this drawing in part 2 when you apply the Disciple's Personality using *James 4:1-8.* View the optional adult *MasterLife* videotape if you need additional help with this presentation. Use the overhead cel you prepared from page 105 for review.

❑ Be prepared to share with students any additional information about the Testimony Workshop. Prepare an overhead cel from page 106.

❑ Contact the person you have trained to be available to help you in the testimony evaluations during this session.

DURING THE SESSION
Part 1 (45 minutes)

Introduction (5 minutes)
1. Greet students as they arrive. Be alert and available to discuss any questions they may have. Begin on time with a prayer.

Testimony Evaluation (20 minutes)
2. Invite students to divide into two small groups. Lead one group while the other group members are led by the person you have trained.

3. Help them focus on their salvation testimony as they write their first drafts. Say, **Testimonies of growth, tithing, prayer, and so on should be used at other times. You are preparing these testimonies for non-Christians.**

4. Each student should list the items he or she added to the basic testimony outline during the work this past week. They will not be sharing full testimonies at this point but are simply discussing the ways they have expanded the basic information and enhanced it from the previous week. Ask them to be brief and factual, with a limit of three minutes per testimony. Write down key words to help you remember points in each testimony. After students give their testimonies, encourage them to take notes as you give brief evaluations. Evaluate the testimony outlines using the following guidelines.
   • Comment on the things that are appropriate.
   • Note things that should be left out.
   • Ask questions to clarify vague areas.
   • Ask about other facts that should be included.
   • Ask other members to give their feedback about key facts in each others' testimonies.
   • Encourage students by expressing your faith in their ability to write the first draft next week.

5. Ask students to tell about their experiences discussing their testimonies with a friend. Ask them to share responses or suggestions made.

6. Close this part of the session by asking students to pray short prayers about the experiences they are having in working on their testimonies.

"My Walk with the Master This Week" (5 minutes)
7. Pair students. Ask them to check each other's "My Walk with the Master This Week." Encourage them to use any extra time to review their memory verses.

"Present Your Body" (20 minutes)
8. Ask, **How do you feel about your body?** (Group response) Say, **State one**

fact about your body that makes you glad. (Group response) Next, state one fact that makes you sad. (Group response) Now, state one fact that makes you mad. (Group response) A lively discussion should follow that will lead to a discussion of this week's study. Depending on students' responses, choose from items 10-12 the activities that relate to their needs. Do not exceed the time allowance.

9. Ask, What are the three functions the body performs in the world? Write them on newsprint or on the chalkboard. Ask for examples that students gave in the activity on pages 156-157 about applying these three functions.

10. Say, Let's talk about the possibility of achieving those applications. What is working against you? (flesh) Who is working for you? (Christ) What three actions of Christ make it possible for your body to be used by God? (incarnation, crucifixion, resurrection)

11. Say, Sometimes it is difficult for you to know how to dedicate yourself to God; but if you present each member of your body to Him as a living sacrifice, it becomes clear. Ask volunteers to share their responses to the first exercise on page 166. Ask for volunteers to share the commitments they made on page 166 to honor Christ with their physical bodies.

12. Ask, Is the body good or evil? Say, In the history of the Christian faith two heresies about the body have arisen. According to both views, the body is presumed to be inherently evil. One group taught that the body was evil and had no relationship to the soul. Thus, people could do anything they wished with their bodies without affecting the spiritual condition. The other group believed that because the body is evil, it must be subdued constantly by beatings, self-denial, starvation, or other means of torture. Ask, What are the implications and consequences of each of these views? What are some contemporary examples?

13. Ask, Can the body sin without the soul being involved? Allow time for discussion. Use Matthew 12:34 and James 1:14-15 to stress the fact that such an idea is ridiculous. A person is a singular, undivided entity. Help students understand that terms such as body, spirit, and soul are used to reflect the different aspects of the total person. Say, If I sin, it is not my mind that has sinned; neither is it my body or my soul. It is I who have sinned and every part of who I am—body, mind, soul, and spirit—is involved.

14. Ask students to volunteer to give testimonies of how applying the incarnation, crucifixion, and resurrection to their daily lives makes it possible for their bodies to be instruments of righteousness. Pray, asking God to help members use their bodies for His glory and purposes.

Take a quick break. Invite youth to help themselves to refreshments.

Part 2 (45 minutes)

Prayer Time (5 minutes)

1. Group together for prayer. Ask volunteers to share a way they recognized during this week's study that they are experiencing victory every day with Christ.

2. Ask for updates on prayer requests mentioned during this study. Lead the group to pray short prayers related to the victories or the prayer requests mentioned.

The Disciple's Personality (20 minutes)

3. Ask students to work in pairs and present the Disciple's Personality to each other. If several students did not give most of the ideas correctly, you may want to give the entire presentation to the group of the Disciple's Personality to refresh their memories. If one member of the pair did not have time to finish, suggest they find a time after the session or during the week to give it. If someone is not able to draw and explain the Disciple's Personality presentation, he or she will need to have you or another member privately meet with them and check his or her presentation before session 12.

4. Begin letting those who are ready to give the Disciple's Personality in its final form do so during this time period. Check off those who do it well. You will have time for only one or two students to present the Disciple's Personality in this session. In week 11 you'll have time to hear the remainder of the presentations.

"In the Carpenter's Shop" (5 minutes)

5. Ask a volunteer to share what is being removed from his or her life and what is being added as the Holy Spirit helps him or her become more Christlike in the area of presenting the body. Pray a prayer of thanksgiving for what this student has shared and for growth that others have experienced.

Training Session (10 minutes)

6. Show your drawing of the Disciple's Personality you made before the session.

7. Ask someone to read *James 4:1-8.* Invite three persons to listen for the source of our struggles in living the Christian life. Invite three others to listen for the solution. Mention that in this passage you will discuss what to do at each moment of temptation to gain victory.

8. Briefly discuss the reports from *James 4:1-8* of the source of your struggles in the Christian life. *(Our lust and desires.)* Say, **Look at James 4:5: "The Spirit Whom He has caused to dwell in us yearns over us—and He yearns for the Spirit** [to be welcome]**—with a jealous love" (AMP).** The Spirit is aggressively concerned about your victory.

9. Discuss the actions Christians take to gain victory. Complete the drawing using the following steps.

- Add *submit* in the space above the word *Spirit,* with an arrow pointing up to God. Beside it write *Draw near to God.* Draw another arrow pointing down from God and beside it write *God will draw near to you.*
- Write the word *resist* in the space below the word *flesh,* with an arrow pointing to Satan. Below the word *Satan* write the result *will flee from you* and another arrow pointing down from Satan.
- Say, **This is the correct order. If you resist Satan in your strength, you will fail. If you first submit to the Lord, you can resist Satan, and he will flee from you. If you send Christ to the door when Satan knocks, Satan will say, "Excuse me; I must have the wrong house." Study these principles in** *Romans 6, 8,* **and** *Galatians 3.*

Next Week's Assignments (15 minutes)

10. Ask students to look at "My Walk with the Master This Week" for week 11 and review the specific assignments. Make sure they understand how to complete each assignment.

11. Briefly preview the content of week 11. Ask students to complete week 11, "Be Filled with the Spirit" before the next session.

12. Ask students to look at "Guidelines for Writing Your Testimony" on page 153 in the student book. Call attention to suggestions that apply to challenges that surfaced during members' discussion of their testimony work. Explain that these guidelines will help them know if their testimony contains all appropriate elements. Instruct them to write a three-minute draft they can read to a small group during next week's session. This would be about 250-300 words or one typed, double-spaced page.

13. Announce any additional information you may have about the Testimony Workshop. Use the overhead cel you prepared earlier showing the Testimony Workshop date, time, and place. Invite questions about the workshop.

14. Call attention to the assignment about writing notes from a sermon on the Hearing the Word form. Say, **Pay attention to applying the message to your life in the week ahead. Be on the alert for sermon references to the theme of being filled with the Spirit, our topic for next week.**

15. Tell students that they will be asked to tell about ways they have used the Disciple's Personality presentation.

16. Remind students of the importance of having each item checked off on "My Walk with the Master" each week to keep these activities from accumulating at the end of the study. Offer individual help outside class if needed.

17. Announce the details for next week's meeting. Close with prayer.

AFTER THE SESSION

❏ Use the following questions to evaluate your group.
  • Do students care for one another? Are they trusting one another? Are they becoming more open with one another?
  • Are there blocks in communication?
  • Are students responding well to my leadership?
  • Is the group becoming cliquish? Do I need to encourage them to keep reaching out?
  • Do some members show undesirable attitudes toward other members? Should I take them visiting together and/or pair them more often?
  • Are students helping disciple one another?
  • Do they see me as a growing disciple who is learning from them?

❏ Continue to invite students to go witnessing and ministering with you. Take them on church visitation or hospital calls.

❏ Call or see all members of the group this week to encourage, enable, or challenge them as needed. See if any need help completing assignments or working on their testimonies. Remember that you are their servant. Continue to look for opportunities to praise them.

❏ Pray for each member. Remember their prayer requests.

❏ Read "Before the Session" for Group Session 11 to evaluate the amount of time you will need to prepare for the next group session. At the beginning of session 11 material, record when you will prepare.

❏ Carefully study week 12 and do all the exercises in the student book. You will preview week 12 for students during session 11.

One-to-One or Mentoring Study Plan

Follow instructions for the Standard Plan. In part 1 help your partner with any problems he or she has related to presenting the Disciple's Personality presentation. In part 2 help your partner organize background material to be used to write his or her testimony for next week's session. When you are presenting the application of the Disciple's Personality, read *James 4:1-8* while the other person listens for the source and solution. Ask for a report as called for. View the optional, adult study *MasterLife* videotape if you feel that would be helpful.

---

[1]From *The Amplified New Testament* © The Lockman Foundation 1954, 1958, 1987. Used by permission.

GROUP SESSION 11

Be Filled with the Spirit

Session Goals

By the end of this session, students will be able to demonstrate their progress toward *MasterLife, Student Edition* goals by...
- completing week 11 assignments;
- answering questions related to the filling of the Spirit;
- using *James 4:1-8* to apply the Disciple's Personality;
- applying a sermon to their lives;
- continuing the process of reading the first draft of their testimonies and receiving feedback;
- making plans for the Testimony Workshop;
- praying for students in their and others' circles of influence.

Standard Plan

BEFORE THE SESSION

❑ Review week 11 and read and complete the learning activities for week 12 of *MasterLife, Student Edition.*

❑ As you complete the study "Be Filled with the Spirit," prayerfully consider whether you are fully experiencing the Spirit.

❑ Pray daily for each member of your group. Some may become discouraged as the amount of work increases before a session. Ask God for guidance and encouragement in each member's life.

❑ Call each member and encourage him or her to attend.

❑ Master this week's material in the Leader Guide.

❑ Review the goals for this session.

❑ Check with the host or hostess to be sure he or she is ready for the group this week.

❑ Arrange the meeting place so that students can sit in a circle.

❑ Finalize plans for the Testimony Workshop. Be prepared to share plans with the group in this week's session. If the workshop is to be held away from the church, prepare a map of the location. Remind students that the workshop will be three hours long.

❑ Have pens or pencils and extra blank paper on hand for the session.

❑ Take notes on a sermon, using the Hearing the Word form on page 220. If you are a pastor, you may want to take notes on a taped sermon or on one preached over the radio or television. You will share with the group your notes on the application of the message. Be specific and open about what needs to be changed in your life.

❑ Draw again on newsprint or the chalkboard the basic picture of the Disciple's Personality. Leave room to add the extra words in the illustration. You will use this drawing when you apply the Disciple's Personality using *Galatians 5:16-25.*

❑ Review "How to Write Your Testimony" on pages 184-186 in the student book. Be prepared to critique students' outlines, using the criteria given in the article and the information in the following section of the Leader Guide.

❑ Contact the person you have trained to help evaluate testimonies. Confirm that he or she will be present for this session.

❑ OPTIONAL: Preview the adult *MasterLife* videotape on how to evaluate a testimony. This will help you evaluate testimonies and give feedback. It will also help you train the other person you enlisted to help you evaluate testimonies.

DURING THE SESSION
Part 1 (45 minutes)

Introduction (20 minutes)

1. Begin with prayer. Ask for requests from group members.

2. Share your experience of taking notes on a sermon this week—including what you wrote in the personal-application section. Be honest about your shortcomings and what you have done or have not done to correct them. Then ask students who are willing to do so to share their notes on how they applied sermons they heard.

3. Ask one or two volunteers to report on the people for whom they prayed in their circles of influence this week. You may need to lead if others don't. Suggest that they not mention names but describe the types of situations in which they encounter these persons. Have a time of prayer in which volunteers pray for concerns that they have voiced about the people for whom they have prayed.

4. Pair members to check each other's "My Walk with the Master This Week." Encourage them to use extra time to review Scriptures they have memorized.

"Be Filled with the Spirit" (25 minutes)

Choose from the following items appropriate questions and activities for your group's study. Do not feel that you have to use each question. Do not exceed your time allowance.

5. Review the content by asking, **How do people know they have the presence of the Holy Spirit within them?** *(If they belong to Jesus.)* Then ask, **How do they know if they have the power of the Holy Spirit?** *(First by faith and then by the fruit and the gifts of the Spirit.)*

6. Call on a volunteer to read *Ephesians 5:18*. Ask, **Which do you consider worse: being drunk with wine or not being filled with the Spirit?** Invite discussion. Emphasize that we are all commanded to be filled; it is not an option for Christians. Point out that the apostles were accused of being drunk on the day of Pentecost. Ask, **Why do you think observers thought the disciples were drunk?** Allow time for discussion.

7. Ask volunteers to describe a time that they have tried to witness on their own strength. What was the result?

8. Review the list of the fruit of the Spirit in *Galatians 5:22-23*. Invite students to find synonyms for the nine nouns. Lead the group to describe a Spirit-filled person in terms of who that person is *(the fruit)* and what that person does *(gifts)*. Be sure they can relate these concepts to aspects of a person's lifestyle.

9. Ask students to read *Ephesians 5:19-20* and identify two results of being filled by the Spirit. *(A Spirit-filled person is characterized by praising and thanking God.)*

10. Ask, **What is the opposite of being filled with the Spirit?** *(Being filled with self.)* Say, **Relate your description of a Spirit-filled Christian to a non-Christian and a worldly Christian.** Ask, **How do they differ?**

11. Select a volunteer to tell about the experience of doing the three things necessary to be filled with the Spirit. Ask the volunteer to express how he or she knows the filling occurred. *(By faith.)* Then ask, **How often will you need to ask for this filling?** *(Daily.)* Emphasize that being filled is not a once-in-a-lifetime experience like salvation. Ask someone who has experienced being filled with the Spirit in previous days to describe how this filling has affected his or her (1) personal character and (2) work for the Lord.

12. Close with sentence prayers of praise and thanksgiving for the fullness of the Spirit.

Take a break. Invite participants to help themselves to refreshments.

Part 2 (45 minutes)

Personal Testimonies (30 minutes)
1. Divide the students into two small groups. Lead one group while students in the other group review Scriptures they have memorized so far in the study.

2. Evaluate the first drafts of their testimonies. Instruct them to be brief and factual, with a limit of three minutes per testimony. Ask each student to read or give the first draft of his or her testimony while others listen.

3. Take notes on the testimony by writing key words or phrases separated by a diagonal slash mark. Put a plus or minus sign or a question mark above each of the words. The plus sign indicates strong material. The minus sign indicates material that should be omitted or improved. The question mark indicates that the member has more material that can be added or material that needs clarification. Your notes might appear as follows.

+   -   +   ?   -   -

Good Home/Age 6/ Fear of Death/ Wreck/Lived 10 Places/Convicted of Sin

Using this note method, you can review the strong and weak parts of the testimony quickly and easily. Tell the student the strong parts first. Then tell him or her how to improve the other parts. Use the criteria given in "Guidelines for Writing Your Testimony" on page 153 in the student book. Keep your notes for the review of the revised version of the testimony next week. Encourage the person who has given the testimony to take notes as you give your brief evaluation. Ask the group to listen to other members' testimonies for ways to improve their own. Encourage them by expressing your faith in their ability to give their testimonies at the Testimony Workshop next week.

4. When you have finished evaluating the testimonies of one group, move to the other. While you are evaluating the testimonies in this group, ask those in the other group to check off each other's Disciple's Personality presentations. (You'll reverse this process in session 12. This provides an opportunity for everyone to give both presentations—the Disciple's Personality and the testimony—in the group.) If necessary, use the person you trained to evaluate testimonies if there is not enough time for you to get around to all students.

The Disciple's Personality (10 minutes)
5. Train students how to apply the Disciple's Personality, using *Galatians 5:16-25*. Show your drawing of the Disciple's Personality. Ask someone to read *Galatians 5:16-25*. Ask three persons to listen for actions Christians should take related to the Spirit. Ask three others to listen for actions Christians should take related to the flesh. Call for reports. Discuss the following actions related to the Spirit.

- *led by the Spirit (v. 18)*   - *live by the Spirit (v. 25)*
- *walk in the Spirit (v. 25)*   - *fruit of the Spirit (v. 22)*

6. Ask students to tell ways they have used the Disciple's Personality presentation.

Next Week's Assignments (5/10 minutes)
7. Ask students to look at "My Walk with the Master This Week" for week 12 and preview the assignments for this session. Make sure they understand how to complete each assignment. Highlight that few new assignments are given to allow time for them to complete all assignments by the next session. Remind them that they will need to have all assignments in their "My Walk with the Master This Week" sections completed by the Testimony Workshop.

8. Briefly preview the content of week 12. Ask students to complete week 12, "Live Victoriously."

9. Instruct students to rewrite the first drafts of their testimonies for the Testimony Workshop, incorporating the suggestions given them during the critique. They may also want to summarize them on a three-by-five-inch card.

10. At the Testimony Workshop students should be prepared to give their testimonies in three minutes. They will give the testimony several times—once to you

and then to persons role-playing a seeker, a self-satisfied person, and a skeptic. Relieve any fears by telling them that those playing the roles will be passive and will not make it difficult for them. They will be able to use their notes on the card if necessary.

11. Call attention to the assignment about writing notes from a Sunday School lesson or a sermon. Urge members to particularly be on the alert for references to the theme of living victoriously, the topic of week 12.

12. Review final details of the Testimony Workshop. Distribute maps, if necessary. Invite questions. Announce plans for transportation to the site, if the workshop is held away from your regular meeting area.

13. Close with prayer. Thank God for the progress students have made. Ask for courage, wisdom, and efficient use of time in the week ahead to prepare for the remaining sessions. Pray that students will be filled with the Spirit continually.

AFTER THE SESSION
❏ Immediately after the session, meet individually or in small groups with those who did not have notes on their personal testimonies critiqued or who had special problems.
  • Suggest why they had difficulty.
  • Show them how to overcome their difficulties.
  • Get them started writing part of it.
  • Keep them working by checking back or by assigning another person to help them during the week.
❏ Send a written announcement about the Testimony Workshop and encouraging each person to be present. Everyone should attend this workshop. Use the sample invitation below.

In acknowledgement of your walk with the Master
during the past six weeks and to celebrate your completion
of weeks 7-12 of MasterLife, Student Edition,
you are cordially invited to attend a Testimony Workshop.
(time • date • place)

Please bring your book indicating your completed assignments and
the final draft of your testimony.

❏ If the retreat is held away from the meeting site, furnish a phone number where students can be reached. Furnish other instructions if they are to bring a sack lunch or other items.
❏ Pray for members as they prepare to present their testimonies.
❏ Take two members with you to minister or to witness. By now you should have taken everyone in the group with you at least once. Perhaps you can visit some of the persons on their prayer lists.

❑ Contact the meeting site for the Testimony Workshop to confirm arrangements for food, lodging, meeting space, and other matters. Arrange for any materials you need for the workshop.

❑ Read "Before the Session" for week 12 to evaluate the amount of time you will need to prepare for your next group session. At the top of the week 12 material record when you will prepare.

One-to-One or Mentoring Study Plan

Follow instructions for the Standard Plan. In part 2 spend time helping the person finalize his or her testimony. Discuss other possible testimonies in addition to the salvation testimony. Discuss when and how a personal testimony may be used. Repeat your testimony as a model. When you are presenting the application of the Disciple's Personality, read *Galatians 5:16-25* while the other person underlines the actions related to the flesh and to the Spirit.

Live Victoriously

Session Goals

By the end of this session, students will be able to demonstrate their progress in achieving the *MasterLife, Student Edition* goals by...
- completing week 12 assignments;
- finalizing plans for the Testimony Workshop;
- sharing successes and failures in living the victorious life;
- sharing ways they have used the Disciple's Personality in their everyday lives;
- sharing ways they have seen other members changed by *MasterLife, Student Edition;*
- continuing to read the first drafts of their testimonies and having them critiqued.

Standard Plan

BEFORE THE SESSION

❑ Review week 12 and read the activities for the Testimony Workshop.

❑ As you complete week 12, "Be Filled with the Spirit," prayerfully consider whether you are living a victorious life in the Spirit.

❑ Pray daily for each member of the *MasterLife* group. Ask God for guidance and encouragement in each student's life.

❑ Call each member of the group to confirm attendance at the final group session and the Testimony Workshop.

❑ Master this week's material in the Leader Guide.

❑ Review the goals for this session.

❑ Check with the host or hostess to finalize plans for the group this week.

❑ Arrange the meeting place so that students can sit in a circle.

❑ Make any last-minute plans for the Testimony Workshop. You will want to share them with group members in this week's session. The next time you meet after session 12 will be for the three hour Testimony Workshop. Provide an emergency number where students can be reached if necessary.

❑ Have pens or pencils and extra blank paper on hand for the session.

❑ Contact the person you have asked to help you evaluate testimonies. Ask them to be present during session 12. Go over item 10 on page 98 with them.

DURING THE SESSION

Part 1 (45 minutes)

Introduction (10 minutes)

1. Greet students and express appreciation for their participation in the group. Begin with prayer.

2. Say, **Share one change you have seen in the life of the person seated to your right since the beginning of weeks 7-12 in** *MasterLife, Student Edition.* Go around the circle until each student has answered.

3. Ask each student to pray and thank God in a sentence or two for the progress in *MasterLife* that the person to his or her left has mentioned about himself or herself.

Verifying Assignments (10 minutes)
4. Pair students to check "My Walk with the Master This Week." Encourage them to use extra time to review Scriptures memorized. All students are to have all assignments checked off by the end of the upcoming Testimony Workshop.

The Disciple's Personality (5 minutes)
5. Ask students to share experiences when they used the Disciple's Personality during the past week.

6. Ask two volunteers to share how they applied *Galatians 5:16-25* to their lives this past week.

"Live Victoriously" (20 minutes)
Choose from the following items appropriate questions and activities for your group's study. Do not feel that you have to use each question. Do not exceed your time allowance.

7. Explain in your own words how the Disciple's Personality explains the possibility of defeat or victory in the life of a disciple.

8. Divide into two groups to discuss the following:
Group 1: In what ways does Satan influence human personality?
Group 2: In what ways does the world influence human personality for good? for bad?

9. Ask the group to summarize how Jesus' death and resurrection bring victory over sin. Then ask, **How important to a victorious Christian life is your crucifixion with Christ?** *(Death to the old person makes possible the new life.)*

10. Ask a student to quote *Galatians 2:20.* Choose a volunteer to recall the two dynamics of victory this verse mentions. *(Death and life.)* Ask, **What motivated Jesus' action on your behalf?** *(He loved you and gave Himself for you.)*

11. Lead a Scripture search of *Romans 6:11-13* to discover three commands that keep you from a lifestyle of sin. *(Think of yourself as dead to sin; don't let sin have control; don't offer any part of your body to sin.)* Ask, **Which of these commands do Christians violate most often?**

12. Encourage students to memorize *1 Corinthians 10:13.* Discuss the difference

between temptation and sin. *(Jesus was tempted but did not sin. Sin is yielding to temptation.)* Ask, **Where does temptation stop and sin begin?** Offer the following analogy: **You cannot stop the birds from flying over your head, but you can keep them from building a nest in your hair!**

13. Point out that when a fleeting, wrong thought becomes a subject that you dwell on and when you let your mind entertain the idea, you have sinned regardless of whether you have acted on the impulse. Read Jesus' example in *Matthew 5:27-28.* Suggest that the following mental discipline is one way of dealing with temptation. Say, **As you are experiencing temptation, picture a cross. Think of Jesus dying on the cross for the very sin you are contemplating. Remember His victory over that particular sin. Thank Jesus for His victory and for your victory.** Ask volunteers to share victories they have experienced recently. Call for testimonies of how they have been able to overcome habits that kept them bound by sin.

14. Review the seven steps to Christlike character on page 218. Make sure students understand the implications of each step. Ask group members to pray silently, thanking God for His forgiveness and cleansing. Then lead a spoken prayer, praising God for Jesus' victory over sin.

Take a break. and invite students to help themselves to refreshments.

Part 2 (45 minutes)

Personal Testimonies (40 minutes)
1. Continue the process you began last week of evaluating personal testimonies. Keep the same divisions you used last week. Lead the group that you did not get to work with while members in the other group check each other's Disciple's Personality presentations. Use the person you trained to evaluate testimonies if there is not enough time for you to get around to all students. As members listen to other members' testimonies, encourage them to make mental notes of ways to improve their own. Encourage them by expressing your faith in their ability to give their testimonies at the Testimony Workshop next week.

Next Week's Assignments (5/10 minutes)
2. Remind students that they will need to have all assignments in their "My Walk with the Master This Week" sections completed by the Testimony Workshop next week.

3. Ask students to rewrite the first drafts of their testimonies, incorporating suggestions given during the critique. Remind them that they can summarize on one three-by-five-inch card. Students should be prepared to give their testimonies in three minutes. They will give the testimony several times—to you and then to persons who will be role-playing a seeker, a self-satisfied person, and a skeptic. Relieve any fears by telling students that those playing the roles will not make it difficult for them. They will be able to use their notes on the card if necessary.

4. Review final details for the Testimony Workshop. Use the cel from page 106 giving the date, time, and place for the Testimony Workshop. Invite questions. Explain transportation arrangements if the workshop is held away from your regular meeting area. Distribute the telephone number where students can be reached.

5. Close with prayer. Thank God for what students have learned about themselves in preparing their personal testimonies. Ask for courage, wisdom, and efficient use of time in the week ahead to prepare for the Testimony Workshop. Pray that each student will be filled with the Spirit continually.

AFTER THE SESSION

❑ Meet individually or in small groups with those who did not have notes on their personal testimonies critiqued or who had problems.
   • Suggest why they had difficulty.
   • Show them how to overcome their difficulties.
   • Get them started writing part of it.
   • Keep them working by checking back or by assigning another person to help them during the week.
❑ Make any final arrangements needed for the Testimony Workshop.
❑ Read "Before the Session" for the Testimony Workshop to evaluate the amount of time you will need to prepare. At the top of the Testimony Workshop material record when you will prepare.

One-to-One or Mentoring Study Plan

Follow instructions for the Standard Plan. Spend extra time helping the other person finalize his or her testimony if needed.

Testimony Workshop

Note to those using the One-to-One or Mentoring Study Plan: The workshop does not work as well with this plan unless several pairs would like to do the training simultaneously. However, you can follow the same step-by-step plan and either find someone to role-play the different persons or play each of the roles yourself. The goal is the same—that the person will be able to master his or her testimony and give it to different types of persons in a role-play situation before giving it in real life. If the person has already been giving the testimony, this session will allow him or her to clarify and sharpen it. As a follow-up, arrange for the person to give his or her testimony in a small group or in a witnessing situation.

Workshop Goals

By the end of this workshop, students will be able to demonstrate their progress toward MasterLife, Student Edition goals by…
- sharing testimonies of growth in Christ during weeks 7-12, of MasterLife, Student Edition;
- completing all assignments in MasterLife, Student Edition;
- revising their personal salvation testimonies to meet the stated criteria;
- adjusting their salvation testimonies to fit the needs of persons playing the roles of a seeker, a self-satisfied person, and/or a skeptic;
- examining ways they plan to seek continued growth in Christ.

BEFORE THE WORKSHOP

❑ Call each member of the group and encourage him or her to attend. Make sure all members understand that they are to bring to this meeting the salvation testimony they have written.

❑ Master workshop material in this Leader Guide.

❑ Review the goals for the Testimony Workshop.

❑ Check on arrangements for the Testimony Workshop. Check the meeting site to be sure it is ready for the group.

❑ Have pens or pencils and extra blank paper on hand for the workshop.

❑ Contact the person you have trained to colead. Make sure

this person knows about workshop arrangements (time, date, place) and what his or her responsibilities are.

❑ Prepare to evaluate each testimony. Review the procedures. Approach your task prayerfully. Scores of potential decisions for Christ may result from this equipping ministry. The attitude you take as you perform this task is important. You are a servant, not a critic. Avoid making students feel they are being tested and can either pass or fail. Lead them to rely on the work of the Holy Spirit as they write and give their testimonies.

❑ Pray for the workshop. Students need to have a sense of accomplishment and success at the end of MasterLife, Student Edition. They will get this from having all their work in "My Walk with the Master This Week" checked off and by successfully completing their written testimonies.

❑ Enlist three people in your church who will agree to play the roles of unbelievers in the Testimony Workshop. Explain the purpose of the workshop and give them the following instructions.

1. Each of you will play one of the roles of an unbeliever: a skeptic, a seeker, or a self-satisfied person. As you role-play, you will wear a three-inch-by-five-inch card with your role name written on the card.

2. Assume the mental state of the particular unbeliever assigned to you. Act out how such a person thinks and speaks.

3. I will make an assignment, or you can choose a role you feel comfortable playing.

4. As you role-play …
   a. Be sincere in the role you play. Respond realistically. It is as insincere to underplay as to overplay the role.
   b. Don't throw any curves at the students. They need positive reinforcement, not discouragement.
   c. Be open in order to draw the students into sharing the testimony.
   d. Spend 3 to 5 minutes with each student and no more than 10 minutes with each team. Expect each person to share their testimony; respond separately to each.
   e. Avoid critiquing the testimony. Simply play the role.
   f. Use concluding comments to reflect your position as an unbeliever but not to reject either the person or the testimony.

Testimony Workshop / 97

Before the session, practice with the role players by playing the part of a student. Present your own testimony to the skeptic; then, let the others assist you in evaluating the way that role player responded. Repeat the procedure with seeker and self-satisfied. This practice will help the role players feel confident when they meet the group.

❑ Prepare the meeting room. Divide a large room into four areas, or use four available rooms for the functions shown in the drawing above. In the first area provide tables, paper, and pencils for members as they work on their drafts. In the second area, provide spaces for you and your coleader to meet with each person to evaluate testimonies. In the third area provide three sets of three chairs. In this section the role players will meet with the teams. In the fourth area provide light refreshments and provide a circle of chairs where members sit for activities not included in the actual testimony time.

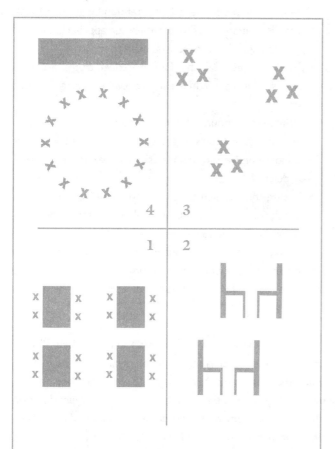

❑ Prepare the following as a printed agenda to be distributed or write it on a poster or chalkboard, or prepare an overhead cel using page 107.

Today's Workshop Agenda
- Have your testimony evaluated.
- Revise it as needed.
- Share it with role players.
- Make adjustments as needed.
- Share final version and/or discuss it with the workshop leader.

DURING THE WORKSHOP
Part 1 (3 hours)

Icebreaker (5 minutes)
1. Greet students as they arrive. Begin on time. Ask members to share the changes they have seen in themselves during this study of weeks 7-12 of *MasterLife, Student Edition*.

2. Pray together. Ask each person to thank God in a sentence or two for the progress group members have made in *MasterLife*.

Verifying Assignments (10 minutes)
3. Ask members to pair up and check assignments for weeks 7-12 of The Disciple's Personality in *MasterLife, Student Edition*. If a member needs a few extra minutes to complete an assignment, arrange to meet with that person during a break in the workshop.

General Instructions (15 minutes)
4. Introduce your assistant for the workshop. Point out that throughout the workshop students should go back to the same leader with whom they start.

5. Introduce the three guest "unbelievers" by their roles (skeptic, seeker, self-satisfied), not by name.

6. Tell students that you will be using "Guidelines for Writing Your Testimony" (student book, p. 160) to evaluate their testimonies.

7. Ask each person to select a partner for the workshop. If this will be a problem, you can appoint them.

8. Call attention to the refreshment area. Suggest that a good time to get refreshments would be when partners are at the work area discussing the experiences they had with one of the role players.

Testimony-Sharing Time (2 hours)

9. Explain the procedure, using the written agenda you prepared.

- Say, **You and your partner will move at your own pace. You are free to change the order of events if a workshop leader or role player is occupied. Use extra time to practice sharing testimonies, complete or review assignments, or recite Scripture you have memorized.**
- Say, **Half of the teams will have their written testimonies evaluated by one workshop leader, and the other teams will have theirs evaluated by the other leader. After reading them, the leader will make suggestions for improvements.**
- Say, **After the testimonies have been evaluated, you and your partner should go to the work area to make adjustments in your testimonies you think are necessary. You may want to make notes on a three-by-five-inch card to use when you give your testimony to the role players.**
- Say, **When you have adjusted written drafts, go to one of the three role players. Partners take turns; one witnesses while the other observes. Each partner opens the conversation with the role player, shares his or her testimony, and concludes with a leading question.**
- Say, **After both of you have witnessed to the role player, return to the work area to evaluate the experience. Discuss difficulties you had and make suggestions to each other. Discuss other facts in "Testimony Outline" (p. 153) that could be used with that type person. Make adjustments necessary to your testimony. Repeat the process with**

the other role players.
- Say, **Finally, you and your partner should share your testimonies verbally with the workshop leader who read your testimonies earlier. Do not use notes unless necessary. Ask any questions that have arisen in the workshop.**

10. This item covers instructions for leaders. Review each person's first draft, asking and answering questions, and making suggestions. Spend approximately 5 to 10 minutes with each person. Let the partner listen so he or she can support the other person. Concentrate on the following areas.

- Look for the story line. Avoid tampering with it, for it tells how Christ entered a person's life. However, if the story line is not present or if it is unclear, the testimony will not sound authentic. In these cases, suggest that it be strengthened in the next draft.
- Examine all parts of the testimony. Are they equally developed? If not, recommend that attention be given to weak areas. If a person is using the thematic approach, the first part does not have to be well developed.
- Check to see that the four doctrinal truths are well expressed in part 3. Make suggestions to strengthen this area.
- Evaluate the amount of detail in the testimony. If it leaves out too many details, suggest other facts be added; if it includes unnecessary details, ask that they be summarized or deleted.
- Be sure the final sentence leads to further conversation.
- Search for church words and religious jargon. The testimony should not sound preachy.

Be available to counsel persons when you are not evaluating testimonies. It is not uncommon during the workshop to have someone receive his or her assurance of salvation or make a decision for Christ.

11. Give a signal when 1 hour is left and again when 30 minutes are left in this period. The latter signal alerts students to share their testimonies with one of the workshop leaders even if they have not shared it with all role players. Stop on time unless agreement is reached by all on extending the session. Another option is to plan a follow-up session.

12. Call the group back together. Thank the role players and give them permission to leave.

Part 2 (45 minutes)

The Spiritual Armor

1. Ask for volunteers to give personal testimonies of what the group and *MasterLife* have meant to them. To get this time started, share your feelings.

2. Encourage students to continue growing in Christ through additional study. Advise them of upcoming youth discipleship opportunities. Assure students that regardless of their decision, you will always be available to talk or pray with them and help them with their life in Christ.

3. Pray for group members. Say, **As I pray, commit to God your decision about continuing further discipleship study. Ask God to speak to you about His will for you.**

4. Close with a prayer of thanksgiving and celebration.

AFTER THE WORKSHOP
❏ Write students expressing appreciation for their participation in the *MasterLife* course.
❏ This is a good time to take stock of the leadership you are providing. If you believe that a problem exists between you and one of the students, visit with this person and clear the air.
❏ Spend time in prayer for each student.
❏ Inform the church of the progress of the group. Ask the church staff when and where some of your students can share testimonies about what *MasterLife, Student Edition* study has meant to them. This is also a good time to enlist members to begin new *MasterLife* groups.

The MasterLife process involves six essential elements. These elements are like the chair pictured.

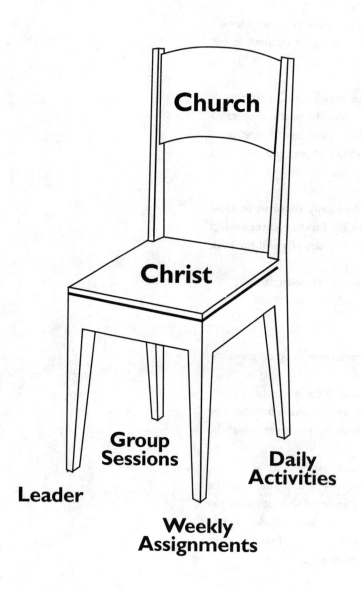

How Jesus Made Disciples

- ABIDE IN CHRIST

- OBEY CHRIST'S COMMANDS

- LEARN BY DOING

- CLARIFY LESSONS LEARNED THROUGH EXPERIENCE

- APPLY LESSONS LEARNED

THE DISCIPLE'S CROSS

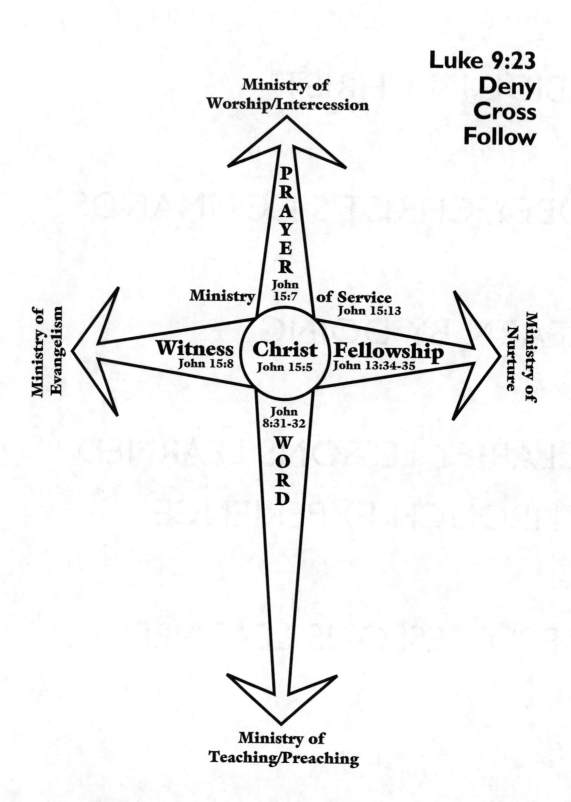

Luke 9:23
Deny
Cross
Follow

Ministry of
Worship/Intercession

PRAYER
John 15:7

Ministry of Service
John 15:13

Ministry of Evangelism

Witness
John 15:8

Christ
John 15:5

Fellowship
John 13:34-35

Ministry of Nurture

John 8:31-32
WORD

Ministry of
Teaching/Preaching

GROWING DISCIPLES WORKSHOP

DATE:

TIME:

PLACE

GROWING DISCIPLES WORKSHOP AGENDA

- The Disciple's Cross

- Discipleship Inventory

- The Disciple's Personality

THE DISCIPLE'S PERSONALITY

The Spiritual Christian

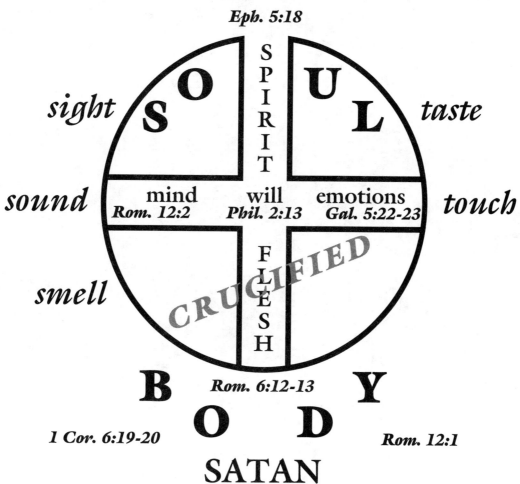

Gal. 2:20
1 Thess. 5:23-24
GOD
Eph. 5:18

sight — SOUL — taste

sound — mind / will / emotions — touch
Rom. 12:2 / Phil. 2:13 / Gal. 5:22-23

SPIRIT

FLESH

CRUCIFIED

smell

BODY

Rom. 6:12-13

1 Cor. 6:19-20   *Rom. 12:1*

SATAN

TESTIMONY WORKSHOP

DATE:

TIME:

PLACE:

TESTIMONY WORKSHOP AGENDA

- Have your testimony evaluated.

- Revise it as needed.

- Share it with role players.

- Make adjustments as needed.

- Share final version and/or discuss it with the workshop leader.

Scripture Memory Verses

Introductory Session: "If anyone would come after me, he must deny himself and take up his cross daily and follow me" (Luke 9:23).

Week 1: "I am the vine; you are the branches. If a man remains in me and I in him, he will bear much fruit; apart from me you can do nothing" (John 15:5).

Week 2: "If you hold to my teaching, you are really my disciples. Then you will know the truth, and the truth will set you free" (John 8:31-32).

Week 3: "If you remain in me and my words remain in you, ask whatever you wish, and it will be given you" (John 15:7).

Week 4: "A new command I give you: Love one another. As I have loved you, so you must love one another. By this all men will know that you are my disciples, if you love one another" (John 13:34-35).

Week 5: "This is to my Father's glory, that you bear much fruit, showing yourselves to be my disciples" (John 15:8).

Week 6: "Greater love has no one than this, that he lay down his life for his friends" (John 15:13).

Week 7: It is God who works in you to will and to act according to his good purpose (Phil. 2:13).

Week 8: I urge you, brothers, in view of God's mercy, to offer your bodies as living sacrifices, holy and pleasing to God—this is your spiritual act of worship. Do not conform any longer to the pattern of this world, but be transformed by the renewing of your mind. Then you will be able to test and approve what God's will is—his good, pleasing and perfect will (Rom. 12:1-2).

Week 9: The fruit of the Spirit is love, joy, peace, patience, kindness, goodness, faithfulness, gentleness and self-control. Against such things there is no law (Gal. 5:22-23).

Week 10: Do you not know that your body is a temple of the Holy Spirit, who is in you, whom you have received from God? You are not your own; you were bought at a price. Therefore honor God with your body (1 Cor. 6:19-20).

Week 11: "Do not get drunk on wine, which leads to debauchery. Instead, be filled with the Spirit" (Eph. 5:18).

Week 12: Do not let sin reign in your mortal body so that you obey its evil desires. Do not offer the parts of your body to sin, as instruments of wickedness, but rather offer yourselves to God, as those who have been brought from death to life; and offer the parts of your body to him as instruments of righteousness (Rom. 6:12-13).

NOTES

NOTES

NOTES

NOTES